W9-BLR-880

MAKING CANADA HOME

How Immigrants Shaped This Country

Revised and expanded edition of *Coming to Canada*, Owlkids Books, 2005

Owlkids Books acknowledges the financial support of the Canada Council for the Arts, the Ontario Arts Council, the Government of Canada through the Canada Book Fund (CBF) and the Government of Ontario through the Ontario Media Development Corporation's Book Initiative for our publishing activities.

Published in Canada by
Owlkids Books Inc.
10 Lower Spadina Avenue
Toronto, ON M5V 2Z2

Published in the United States by
Owlkids Books Inc.
1700 Fourth Street
Berkeley, CA 94710

Library and Archives Canada Cataloguing in Publication

Hughes, Susan, 1960-, author
Making Canada home : how immigrants shaped this country / Susan Hughes. -- Revised and expanded edition.

Previously published under title: Coming to Canada, c2005.
Includes bibliographical references and index.
ISBN 978-1-77147-202-9 (hardcover)

1. Canada--Emigration and immigration--History--Juvenile literature. 2. Canada--Population--Ethnic groups--History--Juvenile literature. 3. Multiculturalism--Canada--History--Juvenile literature. I. Hughes, Susan, 1960- . Coming to Canada. II. Title.

FC608.I4H83 2016 j971.004 C2016-900400-7

Library of Congress Control Number: 2016930942

Updated and edited by: Niki Walker
Designed by: Alisa Baldwin

Canada Council for the Arts Conseil des Arts du Canada

Canada

Manufactured in Dongguan, China, in July 2016, by Toppan Leefung Packaging & Printing (Dongguan) Co., Ltd.
Job #BAYDC25

A B C D E F

Owlkids Books is a division of

MAKING CANADA HOME

How Immigrants Shaped This Country

Susan Hughes

Owlkids Books

CONTENTS

CANADIAN PACIFIC
STEAMSHIPS
to
LIVERPOOL - LONDON
SOUTHAMPTON
GLASGOW
CHERBOURG
ANTWERP - HAMBURG
JAPAN-CHINA
IRCC

Introduction

MAKING CANADA HOME

Did you know that people from every single country in the world have made Canada their home? In this book, you'll read stories about the many people who came to this land and joined with those already here to help make it the vibrant, multicultural country it is today.

Over the centuries, immigrants have come to Canada for a lot of different reasons—to own land, to get work, to escape from poverty or violence, to find adventure, or to reunite with family members already here. Mainly, they all came hoping to build a better life than they could in the country they left behind. And whether they arrived three centuries or three years ago, these newcomers to Canada have faced the task of making this new, often very foreign, place their home. In the process, they helped shape the country.

The story of Canada is a combination of the stories of these countless newcomers, why they came, and how they've made a place for themselves. It is also made up of the stories of those people who were already living here, including how they responded to new immigrants. Although Canada today is known for being a tolerant and accepting place, that has not always been the case. Racism and intolerance are also part of Canada's story, and both have played a role in shaping the country.

This book will tell some of the stories of Canada's immigrants, but nowhere near all of them. There are simply too many for that. All Canadians have important stories to tell of how someone in their family came to be here or how the arrival of newcomers affected them. Some of these stories took place only yesterday, while others stretch back to before the country even had a name.

Canada's history is a long and winding narrative of resistance and acceptance, of discrimination and tolerance, of rejection and welcome. It's a story that is still being written.

Chapter 1

CANADA'S FOUNDING PEOPLES

Every year on July 1, Canadians from coast to coast to coast celebrate Canada Day. The holiday is often described as Canada's birthday, but that makes it sound as if Canada suddenly appeared with Confederation on July 1 in 1867. It didn't. The land itself was already here, of course, and people—in self-governing communities—had been living on it for thousands of years. Others began arriving long before the fur trade, and then came the French and English, and more and more people came to the land before it became a country.

Different people from different places and cultures had a hand in shaping Canada's character along the way to Confederation. As people arrived, they brought with them pieces of the life they'd left behind—cultures, languages, skills, knowledge, and more. They interacted with the land. Many interacted with the people already here, learning from and being shaped by them.

In turn, over time, they made their own contributions. They built homes, farms, towns, and roads. Through trade, these early immigrants laid the foundations for Canada's economy, which attracted even more immigrants. Their ties to their home countries, to their laws, and to their cultures and languages shaped Canada's government, society, and culture. Although the relationship between the founding peoples—Aboriginal peoples, the French, and the English—would remain complicated, conflicts and compromises did result in the 1867 birth of one nation, Canada.

The First Immigrants

When did the first immigrants begin arriving in Canada? Two hundred years ago? Three hundred? Try 12,000 to 30,000 years ago—long before the country of Canada even existed! How did they get here? No one is completely certain, but scientists have a few ideas.

By Bridge...

Many scientists believe that the earliest immigrants were Stone Age hunters who followed animal herds across a land "bridge" from the northern tip of Asia to North America thousands of years ago. If you look at a map showing the Bering Strait, you can see where the bridge would have joined modern-day Siberia with Alaska. Scientists believe this land bridge was there between 75,000 and 14,000 years ago, before the last ice age ended and the melting glaciers flooded the land and left it under water.

...Or by Boat?

Other scientists disagree with the land-bridge theory. They don't think a land bridge ever existed, and even if it did, they maintain that the freezing climate would have made it impossible for people to survive long enough to cross it. Instead, these scientists believe that the first people came by boat from Asia, Australia, or Siberia. Some anthropologists claim that humans were capable of ocean journeys as long as 30,000 years ago. They point out that the sea current running between Japan and the western coast of North America could have made a journey across the Pacific Ocean possible.

Evidence shows that people have been fishing Canada's waters and hunting its coastlines for at least 12,000 years.

These petroglyphs, or rock carvings, were found near Nanaimo, British Columbia. They are thought to be 1,000 years old.

ON THE MOVE

While no one is really sure where the first immigrants to arrive in Canada came from, we do know that people have been on the move all over the world for a very long time. There is evidence that early humans made their way from Africa to the Middle East 100,000 years ago. About 50,000 years ago, people began to spread from there to Southeast Asia and Europe. People travelled by boat to Australia around 35,000 years ago, and almost every corner of the world was occupied by about 8000 BCE. In fact, only a few islands and some extreme environments, like Antarctica, remained uninhabited until more modern times.

Ancestors of Canada's First Peoples

However they got here, the earliest immigrants eventually spread out across the continent and became the ancestors of Canada's Aboriginal peoples—the First Nations, Inuit, and Métis. First Nations and Inuit oral traditions include origin stories that explain how their ancestors came to be on the land. According to these stories, they have been here since the beginning of time and memory.

Canada's First Peoples

First Nations and Inuit were living throughout the land that would become Canada when Europeans "discovered" it in the 1500s. Historians are not sure exactly how many Aboriginal people were living here, but many believe there were at least 500,000. They had formed distinct nations, each with its own culture, society, history, traditions, and way of life.

Living off the Land

One thing all these nations had in common was their self-sufficiency. Canada's First Peoples had developed ways of life that were closely tied to the environments where they lived. The land, plants, and animals provided everything they needed, from clothing and shelter to medicine and tools. Within each First Nation, there were skilled hunters and gatherers, and many people also farmed. They grew crops such as corn, beans, and squash. Canada's First Peoples also traded among themselves for materials that couldn't be found in their area. They had well-established trade routes long before Europeans arrived.

Early European–First Nations Contact

People often refer to the British and French as Canada's founding peoples. But there would be no Canada if it weren't for the First Nations. Their interactions with European explorers and settlers had a lasting impact that helped shape the future of Canada. Many First Nations shared their knowledge of the land,

teaching Europeans which plants were safe to eat and how to use others as medicines. They showed the newcomers how to hunt and fish animals they'd never seen before and how to raise unfamiliar crops. They shared inventions such as the canoe and the snowshoe, which allowed Europeans to travel more easily. And they shared their names for places, plants, and animals—many of which are still used today. Their help enabled the Europeans to survive and establish lasting settlements.

But the positive outcomes of contact were offset by many negatives—for the First Nations. Europeans introduced diseases that First Nations and Inuit people had never encountered, including smallpox, measles, and tuberculosis. These illnesses ripped through many communities, killing large numbers of people and sometimes wiping out entire villages. Europeans also introduced First Nations to alcohol and guns, with devastating results. Over time, as Europeans took over more land, First Nations were forced to rely on trade with the Europeans, and their traditional ways of life changed.

(LEFT) First Nations living near water relied on rivers and lakes for transportation. They developed methods for making sturdy, watertight canoes from birchbark and spruce gum. They also established trade routes along waterways such as the Great Lakes and the St. Lawrence and Mississippi Rivers, allowing them to exchange goods with other First Nations far inland.

(BELOW) Some First Nations hold celebrations called powwows. They feature traditional dancing, music, food, arts, and crafts. This powwow is hosted in Vancouver by the Squamish Nation.

ABORIGINAL PEOPLES TODAY

Today, there are almost 1.5 million Aboriginal people living in Canada. There are hundreds of nations, and more than fifty Aboriginal languages are spoken. Aboriginal languages, cultures, technologies, and social systems have played an important role in shaping the country as we know it. Even the name Canada comes from the Huron-Iroquois word *kanata*, meaning a small village.

European Arrivals

In the 1400s, explorers began sailing from Europe in search of "new" lands, riches, and resources. While looking for a sea route from Europe to Asia, explorers from Spain, England, and France landed on the shores of North America instead. They claimed the places they "discovered" for their countries, even though First Nations and Inuit peoples were already living there.

From Fish to Furs

In 1497, John Cabot became the first European to reach the east coast of Canada since the Vikings, who had settled in Newfoundland for a few years around 1000 AD. While exploring the area, he and his crew found the Grand Banks. The men returned to Europe with stories about the seemingly endless supply of fish, and word of the Grand Banks spread.

By the late 1500s, fishermen from England, France, Spain, and Portugal began making regular trips to Canada's east coast. While they were there, they traded with local First Nations, exchanging metal tools, pots, and other goods for otter, fox, and beaver furs, which they took back to Europe. These men unknowingly started the fur trade, which fuelled European interest in North America.

The Fur Trade

In the early 1600s, beaver felt hats became the rage in Europe, and demand for beaver pelts exploded. The fur trade grew along with the demand. England and France competed for control of it. Explorers and traders went farther into what would become Canada, claiming land as they went. Along the way, both the English and the French formed trade relationships and alliances with First Nations. The British allied with the Haudenosaunee, or Iroquois, Confederacy—the Seneca, Mohawk, Oneida, Onondaga, and Cayuga nations. It was known as the Five Nations. (After the Tuscarora nation joined in the early 18th century, the confederacy also became known as the Six Nations.) The French allied with the Huron, Algonquin, Odawa, Montagnais, and Mi'kmaq nations.

Soon, Britain's territory, known as Rupert's Land, covered 7.8 million square kilometres (3 million square miles) around James Bay and Hudson Bay. France's territory, New France, stretched from the present-day Maritimes along the St. Lawrence River to Quebec and south to Louisiana.

(**LEFT**) The fur trade was the start of a relationship that helped lay the foundations of Canada. Europeans often relied on First Nations guides and their knowledge of long-used trade routes to travel farther into the New World. The maps made by early explorers reflect their Eurocentric view of the world.

(**ABOVE**) L'Anse aux Meadows, in Newfoundland, is the site of the earliest known European settlement in North America. Vikings built it around the year 1000 and probably stayed for a few years.

BIRTH OF THE MÉTIS

Coureurs de bois, or "runners of the woods," played an important role in the early fur trade and in shaping Canada. These men travelled outside European settlements, into the wilderness, where they traded with First Nations for furs. They then sold the furs at British and French trading posts. They formed relationships with First Nations people, living among them, learning from them, and having families with them. The children of *coureurs de bois* and First Nations women were the first Métis. Today the Métis are recognized as one of Canada's three Aboriginal peoples, along with First Nations and Inuit.

The Acadians

In the early 1600s, France aimed to cement its claims to North America—and the fur trade—by establishing colonies in New France. It controlled an area called Acadia, which covered the present-day Maritimes as well as parts of Maine and Quebec. The first French colonists established a colony on an island in what is now Maine, but after a disastrous first winter there, they moved to a spot in present-day Nova Scotia. They named their settlement Port-Royal.

At Port-Royal, the Acadians put up solid buildings and even made dykes to hold back the ocean tides and create rich, fertile farmland. It became a thriving settlement as the settlers farmed and traded with the nearby Mi'kmaq First Nation for furs. Over time, the Acadians developed a unique culture that blended their French heritage with their life in the New World.

In 1755, many Acadians were called to their parish church to hear the order of expulsion read out by British soldiers.

French... British... French...

Port-Royal quickly became an important part of the fur trade, and Britain wanted to control it. For the next 150 years, it passed from French control to British control and back again. During the times Britain had control, Scottish settlers arrived and the area around Port-Royal was renamed Nova Scotia ("New Scotland"). But the Acadians stuck together no matter who was in charge, forging an identity based on their shared language, history, and experiences living on the east coast.

The Great Expulsion

Things took a bad turn for the Acadians in 1755, however. Britain had control of Nova Scotia, and hostilities were rising with France. Britain announced that all colonists had to swear an oath of loyalty to the Crown. Although the Acadians no longer thought of themselves as French subjects, they had no ties to Britain either. When they refused to take the oath, British soldiers rounded them up. Some Acadians escaped, but most were put aboard ships and sent far away. British soldiers burned their homes and farms, and eventually British settlers took over their land.

The Acadians Return

In 1763, hostilities between France and Britain finally ended, and France gave Britain control of New France. The British gave the Acadians permission to return, but not to their old lands in Nova Scotia. Instead, the Acadians who made their way back started over in Cape Breton and other areas of Nova Scotia, as well as New Brunswick. By the time of Confederation, in 1867, there were 87,000 Acadians living in Canada.

(TOP) British soldiers burned the Acadians' farms and houses before forcing them aboard ships and sending them to Pennsylvania, Georgia, South Carolina, and other ports far from their home.

(RIGHT) August 15 is National Acadian Day. Acadians celebrate with a Tintamarre—a lively, noisy parade through their communities.

ACADIANS TODAY

Today, Canada is home to nearly half a million Acadians. They work hard to keep alive their unique, centuries-old heritage. They have their own national anthem, and the Acadian flag flies proudly from many Maritime rooftops. In 2004, Nova Scotia hosted a celebration to mark the 400th anniversary of the founding of Acadia. Hundreds of thousands of people from France, Louisiana, and the rest of Canada came to meet their fellow Acadians and celebrate their common ancestry. Descendants of the Acadians in Louisiana are known today as Cajuns.

The First Québécois

In 1608, Samuel de Champlain, known today as the Father of New France, helped plant deep French roots in the land that became Canada. He sailed down the St. Lawrence River to Quebec, where he found the ideal spot to build a walled fort he called the Habitation de Québec. He believed the cluster of buildings would be the foundation for a permanent, prosperous French colony.

Building a Dream

Working hard to fulfill his dream, Champlain crossed the ocean twenty times to promote Quebec to potential colonists. Slowly, the settlement began to grow. Soon it had a Catholic church, some warehouses, and several homes, in addition to the buildings of the original Habitation. New colonists crossed the sea to make a life in Quebec, and many brought their families with them.

Wars with the Haudenosaunee

Life was not always peaceful in the new colony, however. The French had made enemies of the nearby Haudenosaunee Confederacy in 1609, when Champlain and a few settlers helped their First Nations allies attack a Mohawk village. Afterward, the Haudenosaunee saw the French as a threat, especially because of their alliance with the Huron and Algonquin nations. For years, the Haudenosaunee warred with the French and their allies. In 1663, France sent a regiment of soldiers to defend the colony. After years of war, the French and the Haudenosaunee reached a peace agreement in 1701.

(LEFT) In 1608, Samuel de Champlain supervised the building of his Habitation de Québec, one of the first French settlements in New France.

(ABOVE RIGHT) The majority of the *filles du roi* got married and earned their dowry money within a year of arriving in New France. Millions of French Canadians today can trace their roots to these women.

The *Filles du Roi*

After the soldiers arrived, there were six young men in New France for every woman! Those aren't good numbers when you're trying to grow a population. The king solved the problem by offering unmarried, impoverished young women the chance for a new life in New France. In exchange, the women received clothing, trinkets, and practical items like scissors and combs. When they married in the colony, they were given a dowry of fifty francs or more—about a year's pay at the time. These women came to be called the *filles du roi*, or "daughters of the king." During the 1660s, nearly a thousand *filles du roi* made a fresh start in New France, where they married and had families.

A Distinct Society

The colony that Champlain founded eventually became Quebec City and the territory around it the province of Quebec. Descendants of the French who settled here are known today as French Canadians, or Québécois. Although Britain won control of New France in 1763, it did little to change the French Canadian way of life. In 1791, the British passed a law guaranteeing the French in Quebec the right to continue speaking French, practising the Catholic religion, and following their legal system, which was based on that of France. Left to maintain their traditions and heritage, French Canadians developed a distinct way of life, and today the Québécois are recognized as a distinct society.

The Loyalists

Throughout the 1600s and 1700s, Britain focused mainly on setting up trading posts rather than colonies in Canada. Most British settlers lived in the Thirteen Colonies to the south, in what would become the United States. That changed quickly at the time of the American Revolution (1775–1783), however, when thousands of British colonists came north to escape that war and continue living as subjects of the Crown. These people were known as Loyalists.

Starting Over

After losing the war in 1783, Britain was eager to fortify the territory it still controlled—the land to the north of the Thirteen Colonies, which included New France. It encouraged the Loyalists to move there by offering them free land and free transportation to their new property, as well as supplies such as farming tools, building materials, blankets, seeds, and food for the first three years.

British North America

Between 1783 and 1784, almost 40,000 Loyalists came to British North America, the territory that would eventually become Canada. With so many Loyalists arriving in their midst, the French were uneasy, and after years of war, Britain wanted to keep all its colonists happy. So it divided part of its territory into two new colonies in 1791. Upper Canada (today Ontario) was intended for British settlers who wanted to speak English and follow British laws and customs. In Lower Canada (today Quebec), French settlers could continue following French civil law and practising French customs, as they had before.

Through their numbers alone, the Loyalists helped build a thriving economy. From their years living in the Thirteen Colonies, many were already skilled pioneer farmers who were used to the climate. They were productive almost from the start. Most were optimistic and ambitious, and they saw an opportunity to create a great new society.

SIX NATIONS LOYALISTS

Most members in the Haudenosaunee Confederacy or Six Nations sided with the British during the American Revolution. In return for their support, the British promised to give them back the lands that had been taken from them by Americans. Because Britain lost, however, this land stayed in American hands. For their loyalty, the Six Nations were instead offered land in what is now Ontario. The Mohawk leader Thayendanegea (Joseph Brant) negotiated an agreement that granted his people about 800,000 hectares (2 million acres) on the Grand River. Since then, however, most of that land has been stripped from the Six Nations. Today, the Six Nations Reserve has about 18,600 hectares (46,000 acres).

(TOP) When great ships brought Loyalists to Nova Scotia, many settled around the Bay of Fundy and eventually founded the city of Saint John. They asked Britain to become a separate colony from Nova Scotia. Their request was granted in 1784, and New Brunswick was formed.

(MIDDLE) Not all Loyalists were British. They also included German, Swiss, and Dutch settlers who had joined the British Army during the war. As many as 4 million Canadians today are descended from a Loyalist ancestor. Loyalist roots are celebrated in everything from statues to postage stamps.

(BOTTOM) Thayendanegea (Joseph Brant) was a Mohawk interpreter, spokesperson, and leader. He led many of the First Nations warriors who fought for the British during the American Revolution.

A LOYALIST'S Story

Hannah Ingraham was just four years old when her father left New York to join the British forces fighting in the American Revolution. She didn't see him again for seven years. When he returned in 1783, the family headed north to the safety of the Saint John River valley. In the excerpt below, Hannah recalls their struggles with the Americans and those first brutal months as Loyalists in a new land.

We had a comfortable farm, plenty of cows and sheep. But when the war began and he [her father] joined the regulars they [the American Patriots] took it all away, sold the things, ploughs and all, and my mother was forced to pay rent for her own farm. What father had sown they took away, but what mother raised after she paid rent they let her keep. They took away all our cows and sheep, only let her have one heifer and four sheep...

Mother was four years without hearing of or from father, whether he was alive or dead; any one would be hanged right up if they were caught bringing letters.

Oh, they were terrible times...

[Father] came home on Sept. 13th, [1783], and said we were to go to Nova Scotia [which then included the land that became New Brunswick], that a ship was ready to take us there, so we made all haste to get ready.

We had five wagonloads carried down the Hudson in a sloop and then we went aboard the transport that was to bring us to Saint John. I was just eleven years old when we left our farm to come here. It was the last transport for the season, and had in it all those who could not leave sooner...

We lived in a tent at St. Anne's Point [now Fredericton] till father got a log house raised. He went up through our lot till he found a nice fresh spring of water, he stooped down and pulled away the leaves that were thick over it, and tasted it; it was very good, so there he built his house. We all had rations given us by the Government, flour and butter and pork; and tools were given to the men, too.

One morning when we waked we found the snow lying deep on the ground all around us, and then father came walking through it, and told us the house was ready and not to stop to light a fire then, and not mind the weather, but follow his tracks through the trees, for the trees were so many we soon lost sight of him going up the hill; it was snowing fast, and oh so cold. Father carried a chest and we all carried something and followed him up the hill through the trees.

It was not long before we heard him pounding, and oh what joy to see our gabled end. There was no floor laid, no window, no chimney, no door, but we had a roof at last.

A good fire was blazing on the hearth, and mother had a big loaf of bread with us, and she boiled a kettle of water and put a good piece of butter in a pewter bowl, and we toasted the bread and all sat around the bowl to eat breakfast that morning, and mother said, "Thank God, we are no longer in dread of having shots fired through our house. This is the sweetest meal I have tasted for many a day."

(TOP) This photo shows Hannah Ingraham in 1860.

(BOTTOM) This 1784 Loyalist encampment on the banks of the St. Lawrence River grew into the town of Cornwall, Ontario (then called Johnston). The painting shows people fishing, cooking, and even taking a stroll—anything to pass the time until they received their new land. Hannah and her family would have lived in similar conditions in their camp at St. Anne's Point.

Early Black Settlers

Thousands of black settlers were part of the wave of Loyalist immigrants who arrived in Nova Scotia between 1783 and 1784. Some came as slaves owned by white Loyalists, and they continued to serve their owners in British North America. Other settlers were free blacks who had escaped from their owners in the Thirteen Colonies to fight in the British Army. They came north to claim the freedom and land grants they had been promised in exchange for their military service.

By His Excellency the Right Honorable JOHN Earl of DUNMORE, His
MAJESTY's Lieutenant and Governor General of the Colony and Dominion of
VIRGINIA, and Vice Admiral of the ſame.

A PROCLAMATION.

AS I have ever entertained Hopes, that an Accommodation might have
taken Place between GREAT-BRITAIN and this Colony, without being
compelled by my Duty to this moſt diſagreeable but now abſolutely neceſſary
Step, rendered ſo by a Body of armed Men unlawfully aſſembled, firing on His
MAJESTY's Tenders, and the formation of an Army, and that Army now on
their March to attack His MAJESTY's Troops and deſtroy the well diſpoſed Subjects of this Colony. To defeat ſuch treaſonable Purpoſes, and that all ſuch
Traitors, and their Abettors, may be brought to Juſtice, and that the Peace, and
good Order of this Colony may be again reſtored, which the ordinary Courſe
of the Civil Law is unable to effect; I have thought fit to iſſue this my Proclamation, hereby declaring, that until the aforeſaid good Purpoſes can be obtained, I do in Virtue of the Power and Authority to ME given, by His MAJE-
STY, determine to execute Martial Law, and cauſe the ſame to be executed
throughout this Colony: and to the end that Peace and good Order may the
ſooner be reſtored, I do require every Perſon capable of bearing Arms, to reſort
to His MAJESTY's STANDARD, or be looked upon as Traitors to His
MAJESTY's Crown and Government, and thereby become liable to the Penalty
the Law inflicts upon ſuch Offences; ſuch as forfeiture of Life, confiſcation of
Lands, &c. &c. And I do hereby further declare all indented Servants, Negroes,
or others, (appertaining to Rebels,) free that are able and willing to bear Arms,
they joining His MAJESTY's Troops as ſoon as may be, for the more ſpeedily
reducing this Colony to a proper Senſe of their Duty, to His MAJESTY's
Crown and Dignity. I do further order, and require, all His MAJESTY's Leige
Subjects, to retain their Quitrents, or any other Taxes due or that may become
due, in their own Cuſtody, till ſuch Time as Peace may be again reſtored to this
at preſent moſt unhappy Country, or demanded of them for their former ſalu-
tary Purpoſes, by Officers properly authoriſed to receive the ſame.

GIVEN under my Hand on board the Ship WILLIAM, off NORFOLK,
the 7th Day of NOVEMBER, in the SIXTEENTH Year of His MAJESTY's Reign.

DUNMORE.

(GOD ſave the KING.)

Free but Not Equal

Enslaved or free, Black Loyalists did not have an easy life. Many never got the land grants they'd been promised, and those who did were hardly better off. They continually found themselves at the end of the line for the lumber, tools, seeds, and other supplies promised by the British. The parcels of land they received were usually smaller than the ones given to other Loyalists, and they were located in undesirable spots. The soil was often so poor that farming it was almost impossible, so they had to find jobs to support themselves.

Although many Black Loyalists were skilled carpenters, bakers, and blacksmiths, they were not allowed to practise their trades. They found themselves with no choice but to work as labourers, clearing roads and cutting trees for very low wages. They competed with other

colonists for these back-breaking jobs and were resented for it. Black Loyalists were the targets of racism and violence, and were often forced out of established towns and villages.

Strong Black Communities

Faced with these hardships, Black Loyalists came together and built several strong communities of their own around Halifax, Shelburne, and Guysborough, Nova Scotia. These were bolstered by later waves of black immigrants, especially those who came in the wake of the War of 1812. Within these communities, black Canadians improved their circumstances by helping one another, and together they developed a unique culture that was strengthened by their close ties.

(BOTTOM LEFT) In 1775, the governor of Virginia wrote a proclamation promising freedom to slaves who escaped from American revolutionary owners and fought alongside the British.

(BOTTOM MIDDLE) Forced out of towns by white settlers, Black Loyalists like the woodcutter pictured here formed several communities in Nova Scotia. At its height in the 1790s, Birchtown, near Shelburne, was the largest settlement of free blacks outside of Africa.

(BOTTOM RIGHT) This family walks along a road just outside Halifax. After the War of 1812, 2,000 or more African Americans came to Canada for land and freedom.

CHAMPLAIN'S RIGHT-HAND MAN

Mathieu da Costa was probably the first black person to set foot on the land that would one day be Canada. Born in West Africa, he made his way to Portugal and then came to the shores of the New World as an interpreter for Samuel de Champlain in 1605. Because he spoke both Mi'kmaq and French, da Costa was able to bridge the linguistic and cultural gaps between the explorers and the First Nations people they encountered.

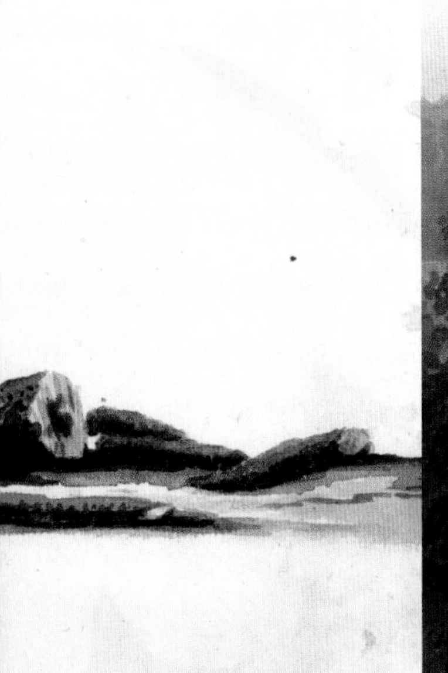

Freedom Seekers

When Britain abolished, or ended, slavery in all its colonies in 1833, British North America became a beacon of freedom for people hoping to escape slavery in the United States. Between the early and middle 1800s, as many as 30,000 African Americans made their way to British North America on the Underground Railroad.

The Freedom Train

The Underground Railroad was a network of people who helped escaped slaves travel north from the United States using secret routes and safe houses where people could hide. People risked serious penalties—even death—by being part of the Underground Railroad, so they used code words to talk about it. "Conductors" helped guide "passengers" to the next "station," while "station masters" offered them a safe place to rest. At the end of the line, British North America was the "terminal" or "Promised Land."

The End of the Line

The Underground Railroad brought "passengers" into British North America all along its border with the United States, but most crossed into Upper Canada (Ontario) along the Detroit River, Lake Erie, or Lake Ontario. When they reached Upper Canada—or Canada, for short—slaves often found they had gained their freedom but not much else. Few white Canadians treated their black neighbours as equals. The former slaves faced discrimination, and they had limited opportunities for work and education.

Help Starting Over

In response to the racism and challenges former slaves often faced, people established a few communities just for new arrivals. These communities not only provided people with support but also offered the chance to farm and own land, to learn a trade, and to go to school. The goal was to provide former slaves with all the skills they would need to succeed in Canada. By the mid-1800s, Canada had its first black doctors, lawyers, and teachers.

THE DAWN SETTLEMENT

Former slave Josiah Henson brought his wife and children to freedom on the Underground Railroad. They reached Canada in 1830, and Henson quickly got to work helping other slaves escape north and improving the lives of those who made it. He founded the Dawn Settlement in Dresden, Ontario, to create a community where former slaves could learn, farm, and work together to develop skills and prosper. The community included the British American Institute, a school where students spent part of their day in a classroom and part learning a trade such as blacksmithing, milling, or manufacturing rope and bricks. It was one of the first vocational schools in Canada.

(ABOVE) The Underground Railroad was run by "conductors." They guided escaped slaves to stops along secret routes, transported them hidden in wagons or carts, and offered them food, shelter, and clothing at safe houses.

(LEFT) Years after he settled in Canada and established the Dawn Community, Josiah Henson wrote his autobiography. It became the basis for a famous American anti-slavery novel, *Uncle Tom's Cabin*.

The Rise and Fall

One of the most successful communities established by African-American immigrants was Africville, in Halifax. Founded in the mid-1800s by families who'd grown tired of working their rocky, thin-soiled lands for little gain, Africville grew to include about 400 hard-working, tight-knit residents. United by their common struggles to earn a living, pay their taxes, and combat racism, the residents drew on one another for strength. Together, they built a community church, school, and post office.

Africville thrived for about 150 years. But Halifax's white community had little regard for it. While the rest of the city gained electricity, water and sewage services, and paved roads, Africville was ignored. When residents asked for the same services found everywhere else, the city council refused. Instead, the city made Africville the site of a prison, a hospital for infectious diseases, a slaughterhouse, and a garbage dump—the undesirable institutions and businesses no one wants in their part of town.

# of AFRICVILLE

How does a community remain strong in the face of such challenges? "We found ways to survive the discrimination," said Irvine Carvery, head of the Africville Genealogy Society. "Our resolve and our strength came from our strong religious beliefs. This held people together during those very difficult times."

But despite the community's inner strength, it all came to an end in the 1960s. Halifax city officials decided to demolish Africville. Residents were offered money to leave their homes, and those who refused to go were simply evicted. Bulldozers came during the night, and personal belongings were moved to public housing complexes in the back of dump trucks. The community that African Canadians had built and loved for more than a century and a half was destroyed.

In 2002, the spot where Africville once stood was named a National Historic Site. And in 2010, after former Africville residents threatened the city of Halifax with a lawsuit, a settlement was reached. It included land and money to help rebuild the church that was bulldozed decades earlier. But to some former residents, it's not enough. They are seeking individual compensation for their land and for the destruction of their community and businesses.

"Many people believed that when the physical structure and buildings of Africville were gone, the spirit would die," said Carvery. "But it hasn't died. Instead of dying away, in fact, the community, and the unity around the community, has grown… The people of Africville still speak with a common voice."

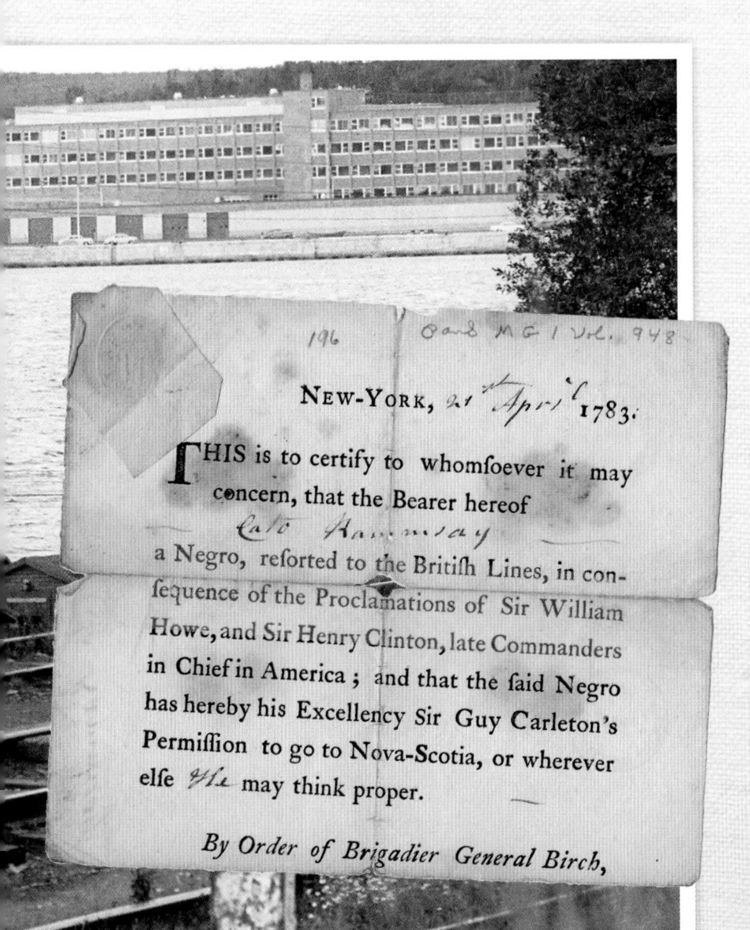

NEW-YORK, 21st April 1783.

THIS is to certify to whomſoever it may concern, that the Bearer hereof Cato Ramsay a Negro, reſorted to the Britiſh Lines, in conſequence of the Proclamations of Sir William Howe, and Sir Henry Clinton, late Commanders in Chief in America; and that the ſaid Negro has hereby his Excellency Sir Guy Carleton's Permiſſion to go to Nova-Scotia, or wherever elſe He may think proper.

By Order of Brigadier General Birch,

(FAR LEFT) Africville became the dumping ground for Halifax's least desirable institutions and businesses. There was even a railway line right through the middle of the neighbourhood.

(LEFT) This certificate of freedom gave Cato Ramsay the right to go to Nova Scotia, "or wherever else he may think proper." Settlers like him helped establish several communities of free blacks in the province.

The British Wave

British immigrants began arriving in eastern Canada in the 1600s, but aside from the Loyalists, they didn't arrive in huge numbers. It wasn't until the mid-1800s that a wave of settlers from England, Scotland, and Ireland began arriving. With the Industrial Revolution fully under way, cities in Britain had filled with people moving from the countryside to find work. Seemingly overnight, cities grew to bursting. People faced overcrowding, dirty living conditions, and shortages of clean water. Hoping for new opportunities and a better life, thousands of people left for British North America.

British North America Becomes Mostly British

Because they came in large numbers, these settlers had a huge impact on their new home. They helped towns and cities grow, and they pushed into new areas, moving the frontier of British North America farther and farther west—and deeper into First Nations territories. Their arrival tipped the British population of British North America into a majority for the first time. By establishing their values, customs, and way of life here, the British settlers cemented the British nature of the territory.

Home Children

The problems in Britain's growing cities affected thousands of children directly. At the

time, children as young as four worked twelve to fourteen hours a day, often in dangerous places such as mines and factories. Many found themselves on the streets because their parents could not afford to keep them. Some were orphans. Thousands wound up living in shelters and orphanages, which were known as Homes. Childcare agencies began arranging for groups of these children, known as Home Children, to immigrate to Canada for the chance of a new life.

No Home Sweet Home

The program had been set up to give orphans a better life, but too often these children were treated as a source of labour and not as a member of the family. And it turns out that most of these supposed orphans actually had parents. They had been sent to Canada anyway—often without their parents' permission—because officials believed they would be better off in a land of fresh air and rolling green fields than in the filthy streets of Britain's cities.

Home children made up one of the largest groups of British immigrants in the 1800s. More than 100,000 came to Canada between 1869 and 1939 from childcare organizations in England, Wales, Scotland, and Ireland. Most settled in Ontario. More than 1 million Canadians are descendants of Home Children.

(LEFT) After arriving, these home children were assigned to families. They would have worked as servants in homes or as labourers on farms in exchange for room and board.

(RIGHT) These boys are learning to farm by working on the Philanthropic Society Farm School, in England. From there, they would be sent to work on farms in Canada and other British colonies.

The Famine Irish

In the mid-1800s, Ireland faced even more problems than the rest of Britain. Cholera swept the country in 1832, and between 1845 and 1848, disease wiped out the potato crop—the main source of food for the island's poor farmers. They began to starve, and year after year the death toll mounted. Almost a million Irish would eventually die in the Great Famine. Desperate to escape, 2 million people had left Ireland by 1850. As many as 400,000 made their way to British North America. They came to be called the Famine Irish.

The Coffin Ships

Irish immigrants made their way to Canada packed aboard cramped, rickety ships that weren't built to carry passengers. The unclean, overcrowded conditions were perfect for typhus, a contagious and deadly disease that spread like wildfire through the ships. As many as 8,000 immigrants died on the trip to Canada.

Steady Work in the Cities

Because of the hardships they'd faced, the Famine Irish became linked in many Canadians' minds with poverty and disease. Outside of Quebec, where Irish Catholics found a relatively warm welcome, few people wanted to hire them for anything but the lowest-paying jobs.

Frantic to feed their families and keep a roof over their heads, Irish immigrants took whatever work they could get. Most were reluctant to farm, given their experiences in Ireland, so they mainly settled in towns and cities, where they found jobs as labourers. By the late 1800s, the Irish were the largest group in just about every town and city outside of Quebec City and Montreal. Today, roughly 14 percent of Canadians claim Irish descent.

MADEMOISELLE...O'REILLY?

Imagine arriving in a foreign country where you don't understand the language, you don't have anywhere to go, and you are all alone. When their parents were killed by the typhus outbreaks on the "coffin ships," hundreds of Irish children faced that situation by the time they reached Quebec. Fortunately, many kind-hearted Quebec families were waiting to welcome them into their farmhouses and cottages. Out of respect for the children's heritage and their deceased parents, the French families who adopted them allowed them to keep their Irish names. Even today, Quebec is home to many proud French-speaking O'Reillys, O'Sheas, and Sullivans—the direct descendants of those original young Irish immigrants.

(ABOVE) These immigrants are patiently awaiting the medical exams that they are required to take before being allowed to enter Canada. If they show any signs of disease, they will need to be quarantined until they are well again.

(LEFT) This replica of the ship the *Jeanie Johnston* shows what it was like for Irish immigrants making their way to Canada in the 1850s. For weeks, passengers lived in cramped bunks like these.

QUARANTINE ISLAND

In the 1800s, most immigrants arrived in eastern Canada from Europe aboard ships, and Quebec City was their main port of entry. To help contain the outbreak of diseases like typhus and cholera, the government built a quarantine station on the deserted island of Grosse Île, in the St. Lawrence River.

Ships arriving from overseas had to dock at the island for inspection. Immigrants who showed any signs of illness were sent to the quarantine station to wait out their sickness—anywhere from a few days to a few weeks.

The station was built with enough room to house 150 people, and for years it worked well. When the "coffin ships" began arriving from Ireland in early 1847, however, Grosse Île became chaos. With so many ships loaded with sick passengers docking each day, the station soon became dangerously overcrowded.

There were not nearly enough attendants to care for everyone, so sick people were put into "fever sheds," with only straw for bedding. The straw was rarely changed or disinfected, even after someone died on it. Eventually, even the immigrant ships themselves became miniature quarantine stations. Sick, dying, and dead passengers were contained inside the ships at anchor, alongside people who were healthy. Many healthy families—wanting to stay that way—chose to sleep on the shore rather than risk infection in any of these shelters.

At the height of the typhus outbreak—the summer of 1847—between fifty and a hundred people died daily. Many doctors, priests, and nuns who'd come to tend the sick also fell victim to the disease. Six men were employed to do nothing but dig graves every day.

For decades after the outbreak, Grosse Île remained the point of arrival for most immigrants who sailed across the Atlantic Ocean for the eastern shores of Canada. As knowledge of diseases and how they spread increased, it became a better, safer place to pass through. The island was divided into sections to keep sick immigrants apart from healthy ones. A laboratory was set up to make testing for disease quicker and easier. And ships and baggage were disinfected to keep any outbreaks under control.

The quarantine station at Grosse Île was shut down in 1937. In 1984, the island was recognized as a National Historic Site. Today, visitors can see the historic buildings, the burial grounds, and the memorials that honour the thousands of immigrants who entered Canada through this forlorn spot.

(TOP RIGHT) The Disinfection Building was built on Grosse Île in 1892. When passengers arrived, they had to shower in a mercury solution to kill any germs on their bodies. While they did, their clothing and luggage were steamed in these compartments.

(BOTTOM RIGHT) This second-class hotel was one of several that were eventually built on the island. They offered more comfortable accommodations for passengers who showed no signs of illness during their quarantine.

Grosse Île's monument to the Irish typhus victims is a Celtic cross, a traditional Irish symbol of the cycle of life.

Removing the First Nations

The flood of British immigrants in the early 1800s into eastern Canada had a huge impact on the First Nations. Non-Aboriginal people soon outnumbered First Nations around the Great Lakes.

With more and more immigrants arriving, settlers pushed even farther into First Nations' territories. First Nations were forced to negotiate treaties, or agreements, with the government. The first agreements offered payments in exchange for allowing settlers to move onto these lands. Later agreements also included land reserves—areas set aside specifically for First Nations people. First Nations people kept their right to hunt and fish on the land forever.

Broken Promises

The First Nations and the government had different views of the treaties they had made. The First Nations believed they had agreed to share their lands, since no one could ever own them. The government saw each treaty as a bill of sale. These differences, along with a series of broken promises by the government, have led many people to see the treaties as unjust.

A New Relationship

The way the government viewed First Nations began to change in the early 1800s. The fur trade was less important, so old trading alliances were less important too. Since Britain had made peace with the United States after the War of 1812, the government no longer saw First Nations as valuable military allies. Instead, they were now only seen as an obstacle to expanding the country and its "British-ness."

"Civilizing" First Nations

In the 1820s, the government started programs to "civilize" First Nations people—to have them abandon their traditional lifestyles for a more British way of life. After Confederation in 1867, the government took this superior attitude even further, taking control of nearly every aspect Aboriginal peoples' daily lives. No one considered—or even asked—what they wanted.

Residential Schools

In an attempt to erase all traces of Aboriginal peoples' language and culture, the government created programs like the residential school system. Under this system, which began in the 1870s, thousands of Aboriginal children were taken from their families, sent to live in schools far away, and punished for showing any trace of their Aboriginal roots. Many were severely abused. This system, which continued well into the twentieth century, was devastating for Aboriginal peoples and their communities.

(TOP RIGHT) Starting in the early 1800s, the government began trying to assimilate First Nations people into a more European lifestyle. It encouraged them to take up farming on reserves.

(MIDDLE) This map shows the lands affected by the Robinson-Huron Treaty and the Robinson-Superior Treaty, which the government and Ojibwa nations in the area signed in 1850. These treaties were the first to set up reserves for the First Nations. They became a model for later treaties, such as the Numbered Treaties.

(BOTTOM) In 1998, the government apologized for residential schools, and in 2001 it began taking steps to compensate survivors. It also set up the Truth and Reconciliation Commission to interview survivors with the goal of developing a new and better relationship with Aboriginal peoples.

Chapter 2

BUILDING THE NATION

On July 1, 1867, the provinces of New Brunswick, Nova Scotia, Ontario, and Quebec officially became a new country—the Dominion of Canada. As a new country, Canada had a lot of work to do—and a lot of opportunities to offer. Prime Minister John A. Macdonald wanted to see the country's borders stretch "from sea to sea." To reach this goal would require making agreements with Aboriginal peoples in the West. It also required a lot of workers, from farmers to construction labourers, and a lot of people willing to settle the land.

Canada didn't have nearly enough people for that, so the government set its sights on attracting immigrants. The country's doors weren't open to everyone, however. To reinforce Canada's "British-ness," the government wanted immigrants from Britain first and foremost. When there weren't enough of those, it eventually opened the doors to include immigrants from other parts of Europe and from parts of Asia. The government thought the Europeans would make good farmers, and it saw Asian immigrants as a source of cheap labour.

Between 1867 and 1914, Canada's population exploded from about 3.5 million to more than 7 million, as immigrants poured into the country looking for work, land, and a chance to prosper. They brought with them their cultures, languages, and traditions, laying the foundations for Canada's multicultural mosaic.

DOMINION OF
CANADA
RIMENTAL FARM,
BRANDON,
TOBA, CANADA.
EXPERIMENTAL FA
INDIAN HEAD
NORTH WEST TERR
RIVER VALLEY,
atchewan Valley,
AT FERTILE PLAINS
itish Columbia
CONTAIN
SUITABLE FOR GRAINS AND GRASSES
MINERAL RICHES
PER, IRON, COPPER, SALT,
ROLEUM, ETC., ETC.
se Coal Fields,
BLE SUPPLY OF CHEAP FUEL.
from Ocean to Ocean.
SEE REPORTS O
BRITISH TENANT FAR
WHO VISITED CANADA
CLIMATE T
HEALTHIES
IN THE WOR
CANADA HA
5 Experimental F
representative of the whole
area of the Dominion, instit
the advancement of Agric
NORTH PACIFIC
OCEAN
ATLANTIC
AFRICA
AUSTRALIA
SOUTH PACIFIC
TABLE OF DISTANCES.
TABLE OF DISTANCES.
CENTRAL EXPERIMENTAL FARM,
OTTAWA, CANADA.
EXPERIMENTAL FARM
NAPPAN, NOVA SCOTIA.
EXPERIMENTAL FARM,
AGASSIZ, BRITISH COLUMB
REE FARMS OF 160 ACRES
Given to every Male Adult of 18 years and over, in the great Fertile Belt of
MANITOBA, CANADIAN NORTH-WEST AND BRITISH COLUMBIA
Deep soil, well watered, wooded, and richest in the world—easily reached by railroads. Wheat—average 30 bushels to the acre, with fair farming.
VAST · COAL · FIELDS · AT · CONVENIENT · DISTANCES
ANTS FROM 100 TO 200 ACRES ARE OFFERED IN OTHER PARTS OF CANAD
Further and full information, in pamphlets and maps, given free on application by letter (within the Dominion, post free,) addressed—
Or to HIGH COMMISSIONER FOR CANADA,

Opening the West

In 1870, the new Dominion of Canada bought Rupert's Land and the North-Western Territory from the Hudson's Bay Company. It was a massive area stretching from Ontario's border to British Columbia and north to the Arctic Ocean. At the time, the land was home to Aboriginal peoples, scattered trading posts, and a few British settlements.

There was some concern that the United States would try to move into the mostly empty area and take it over. Canada's government wanted to make it clear that this land was spoken for. In 1871, it began negotiating a series of agreements called the Numbered Treaties with First Nations in the West. The treaties basically stripped the First Nations of their lands, clearing the way for newcomers.

Free Land

In 1872, the government passed the Dominion Lands Act in the hopes of luring immigrants to the prairie grasslands to build homesteads. It offered 65 hectares (160 acres) to anyone over the age of twenty-one who paid a ten-dollar registration fee. Homesteaders had to live on their land for three years in a row, farm at least 12 hectares (30 acres), and build a permanent house. Once they'd done all that, the land was theirs.

The Dawson Route

Settlers wanting to claim free land faced a lot of hurdles just getting to it. There was no railway to the West until the mid-1880s. The only way to get there was via the Dawson Route, which ran from present-day Thunder Bay to Winnipeg—a trip of about 850 kilometres (530 miles). The journey was a combination of steamboats and bumpy ox-cart rides along a road that was little more than a trail. From start to finish, people had to load and unload their belongings seventy times. The trip was long and exhausting—and enough to discourage all but the most determined settlers.

Not Many Takers

It's not surprising that immigrants didn't rush to settle the Prairies, despite the offer of free land. Instead, they poured into the American West by the thousands. The United States had a railway, a milder climate, and a similar offer of free land. A few groups, including Icelanders, Mennonites, and Hungarians, did head for Canada's West, however. Most were lured by the promise that they would be left to build and run their own communities as they wished.

(TOP LEFT) Throughout the 1870s and 1880s, the government advertised its promise of 160 acres (65 hectares) to people in Britain, northern Europe, and the United States.

(TOP RIGHT) This 1893 receipt from the Dominion Lands office shows that a settler had paid his fee and was entitled to a lot somewhere near Calgary.

(BOTTOM) This family of German immigrants settled in Saskatchewan in the 1880s. They were the first to receive a homestead title in what eventually became the town of Strasbourg.

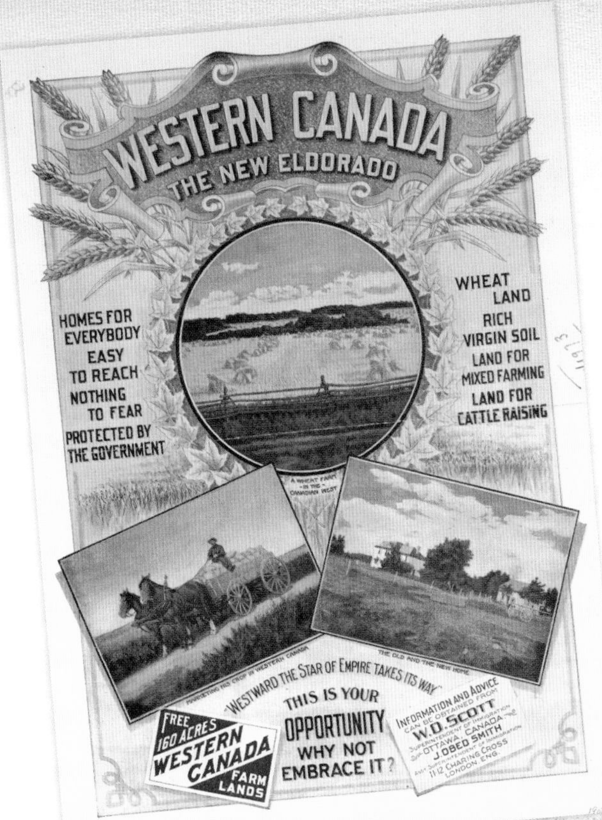

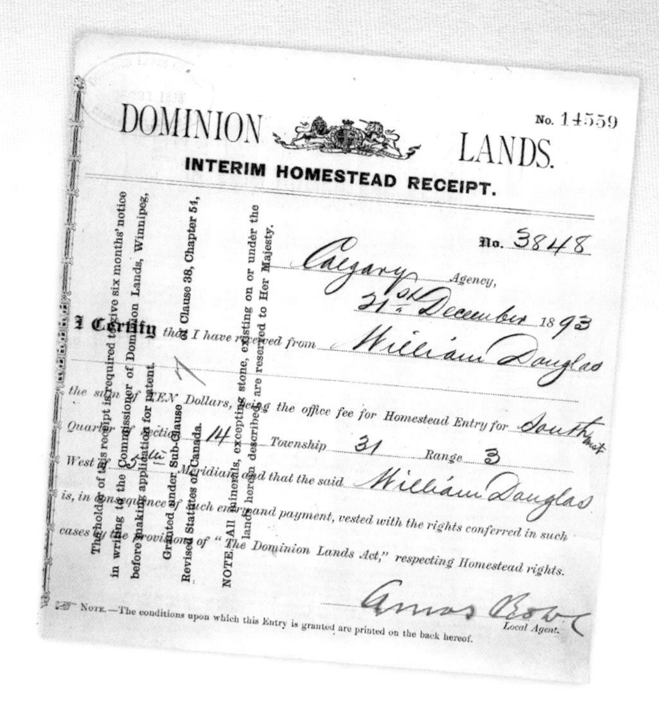

DOMINION LANDS. No. 14559

INTERIM HOMESTEAD RECEIPT.

No. 3848

Calgary Agency,

21st December 1893

I Certify that I have received from William Douglas the sum of TEN Dollars, being the office fee for Homestead Entry for South West Quarter of Section 14 Township 31 Range 3 West of 5th Meridian, and that the said William Douglas is, in consequence of such entry and payment, vested with the rights conferred in such cases by the provisions of "The Dominion Lands Act," respecting Homestead rights.

Amos Bowe
Local Agent.

The holder of this receipt is required to give six months' notice in writing to the Commissioner of Dominion Lands, Winnipeg, before making application for patent.

Granted under Sub-Clause 1 of Clause 38, Chapter 54, Revised Statutes of Canada.

NOTE. All minerals, excepting stone, existing on or under the land herein described are reserved to Her Majesty.

NOTE.—The conditions upon which this Entry is granted are printed on the back hereof.

The Mennonites

In 1874, a group of about 7,000 Mennonites became the first overseas immigrants to arrive on Canada's Prairies. The Mennonites had chosen to leave the Ukraine, which was part of the Russian Empire, because Russia began requiring schools to teach in Russian and citizens to serve in the military. As German-speaking pacifists, the Mennonites were unhappy with these changes. They settled on Canada as their new home after the government promised that they would be free to practise their religion, to live in their own communities separate from mainstream society, and to refuse military service.

The Mennonites settled in two colonies close to Winnipeg. Although the Dominion Lands Act required settlers to live on and farm their properties, the government agreed to let the Mennonites set up communal villages on the land they had been granted.

Traditional Villages

To form a village, about twenty families combined their homesteads into a large shared plot. They built a main street, or *Strassendorf*, along which each family built a house and an attached barn. They also built community buildings like a church and a school. The families then pooled all the surrounding land and divided it based on what it was best suited for: pastures for livestock, farmland for crops, and woodland for lumber and firewood. Every family got a share of each type of land.

(BELOW LEFT) These Mennonite farmers are working together to thresh a crop of wheat in Manitoba.

(BELOW RIGHT) Mennonite settlers built houses with barns attached like this one in Winkler, Manitoba.

Everyone Did Their Part to Prosper

The settlers worked hard to establish their villages. When they first arrived on the empty plain, they slept under their wagons and quickly built temporary shelters to get them through the first winter. They dug wells and cleared enough land to plant a crop that would feed them that first year.

For the next couple of years, they worked tirelessly. Within three years, they had expanded their fields, built their large housebarns, and raised enough livestock that they had extra meat, eggs, and chickens to sell at the market in Winnipeg. Everyone in the village did their part, and together they became some of the most successful Prairie farmers.

MENNONITES TODAY

Today, almost 200,000 Mennonites call Canada home. With 20,000 Mennonites, Winnipeg has one of the largest urban Mennonite populations in the world. Other cities with large Mennonite populations include Kitchener-Waterloo, Vancouver, and Saskatoon. All these cities also have large rural Mennonite populations nearby.

(ABOVE) Some Mennonites, known as Old Order or Amish, choose to live without electricity, cars, and other modern conveniences. Many are farmers who sell their goods at local markets, such as the St. Jacobs Market, which is near Kitchener, Ontario.

The Icelanders

In 1872, Sigtryggur Jónasson became the first Icelander to set foot on this land since the Norse explorers built L'Anse aux Meadows in the eleventh century. At the time, his island home was plagued by disease, famine, and devastating volcanic eruptions that spewed ash, destroying homes and pastureland. He hoped to start a colony in Canada that would be a "new" Iceland, a place where Icelanders could stay together, speak their language, keep their customs, and prosper.

A Little Piece of Iceland in a Foreign Land

Jónasson convinced other Icelanders to follow him. They tried to set up a couple of colonies in the east, without success. Then, in 1875, the government sent Jónasson and two other Icelanders to the new province of Manitoba to scout possible locations. The government promised the men an area of land that Icelanders could govern as their own. When the adventurers arrived on the shores of Lake Winnipeg, they found abundant fish, fertile soil, and forests they could use for timber and fuel. They had found their new home, which they called Nyja Island, or New Iceland.

New Iceland

On October 21, 1875, a group of 235 hardy Icelanders arrived in New Iceland. Their first winter was tough. Some of them had never seen a tree, yet they had to clear many acres of land. They figured out how to hunt, how to handle unfamiliar tools, and how to cook with unfamiliar foods, using a sweet sap for sugar and wheat kernels for coffee. They set up tents, built shelters for several families to share, and even raised a school that first winter. On top of all that, the settlers drafted a constitution and laws for the colony, and set up a council to administer them.

Jónasson, meanwhile, returned to Iceland to attract more settlers. Almost 1,200 came in 1876. But the colony faced several hardships over the years, and many colonists left for Winnipeg. By 1881, there were only 250 people left in New Iceland. They held on, however, and by 1900 the colony's population had climbed to 2,000. The New Icelanders had succeeded in building a colony, one of the first European settlements in Canada's West.

Maintaining Traditions

Creating their own settlement allowed Icelanders to maintain many elements of their traditional culture, language, and society, even as Canada grew around them. Today, there are about 180,000 Canadians of Icelandic descent, and Manitoba is home to the largest Icelandic population outside of Iceland.

(TOP RIGHT) Sigtryggur Jónasson was just twenty when he became the first modern-day Icelander to travel to Canada. He came to be known as the Father of New Iceland.

(MIDDLE RIGHT) In 1875, more than 200 Icelandic men, women, and children travelled from Winnipeg to a new colony on the shores of Lake Winnipeg.

Lake Winnipeg was important to the new settlers, many of whom were experienced fishermen. At first the settlers, who were used to deep-sea fishing, had trouble bringing in a catch. Eventually they adapted their skills, however, and fishing became the colony's main industry.

Linking the Country

After Confederation, one of the government's first big projects was building a railway to link the east coast with the west coast. The railway would help attract more settlers and grow Canada's economy by making it easier to move people and goods across the country. And it was part of the deal the government made with British Columbia when that province joined Confederation in 1871.

By 1880, however, British Columbia's section of the railway still had not been built, and the situation was causing headaches for politicians from one coast to the other. The province remained cut off from the rest of the country—and Canada was running out of time to fulfill its promise.

Desperate Times

The minister of railways, Sir Charles Tupper, was feeling the pressure. Desperate, he turned over the railway and its construction to the Canadian Pacific Railway Company. It hired Andrew Onderdonk, an American contractor and engineer, and asked him to oversee building the rail line through British Columbia, from Port Moody to Craigellachie.

This section involved the difficult, dangerous task of laying track through hundreds of kilometres of mountainous terrain. Onderdonk realized immediately that he would need far more workers than he could find locally, and the cheaper the labour, the better.

When the Canadian Pacific Railway was finally finished, it did exactly what it was supposed to—unite the country from one end to the other. This photo shows the first train to travel all the way from the Atlantic to the Pacific.

Chinese Labour

Onderdonk decided that the only way he could complete the job was by bringing in Chinese labourers, who worked for much lower wages than other workers. When he announced his plan, however, the people of British Columbia reacted angrily. They didn't think it was fair for foreigners to take jobs from Canadians—even though this was dangerous work that few Canadians wanted to do—and they were nervous about living alongside people who seemed so different. But Onderdonk stood firm. If he was not permitted to recruit Chinese workers, he warned, the rail line would take twelve more years to complete! In the end, the government gave him the go-ahead.

(ABOVE) This statue near Toronto's CN Tower is a monument to the work and sacrifice of Chinese railway labourers who played an important role in linking this country from coast to coast.

(LEFT) This photograph shows Donald A. Smith, a major backer of the Canadian Pacific Railway, driving home the Last Spike. It is meant to represent the completion of the railway, and it's one of the most famous photographs in Canadian history. But the Chinese labourers who actually laid much of the western track are nowhere to be seen.

Early Chinese Immigrants

Between 1881 and 1885, 17,000 Chinese labourers made the enormous decision to leave their homes and families and cross the Pacific Ocean to British Columbia to work on the railway. Most were peasant farmers looking to escape from poverty and high rents. They wanted a chance to work hard, earn money, and build a better life.

Working on the Railroad

Their dreams for a better life disappeared quickly in the reality of Canada's railway camps. After fifty long days at sea, the workers were put to work as soon as they arrived. They were given the most back-breaking and treacherous jobs high up on the sides of mountain valleys, where one wrong step could start a landslide or plunge them to their deaths. The most dangerous task was placing the highly unpredictable liquid explosives used to blast out sections of mountain. Chinese workers almost always did this job. Is it any wonder that about 4,000 of them died building the railway?

For risking their lives, the Chinese workers earned just a dollar a day—half what white labourers earned. They paid for their camp gear, food, and clothing from their earnings, while these supplies were provided to white labourers for free. This racist treatment was just a glimpse of what would come in their new home.

No Longer Needed

When the Canadian Pacific Railway was completed in 1885, thousands of Chinese men found themselves out of work. A few returned to China, but most could not afford the trip. Some headed to towns and cities to the east, but the majority stayed in British Columbia. Many found work in sawmills and fish canneries, which had sprung up as the lumber and fishing industries grew. Once again, they did the most dangerous jobs and were paid less than other workers. White Canadians resented the Chinese workers and blamed them for lowering wages for everyone.

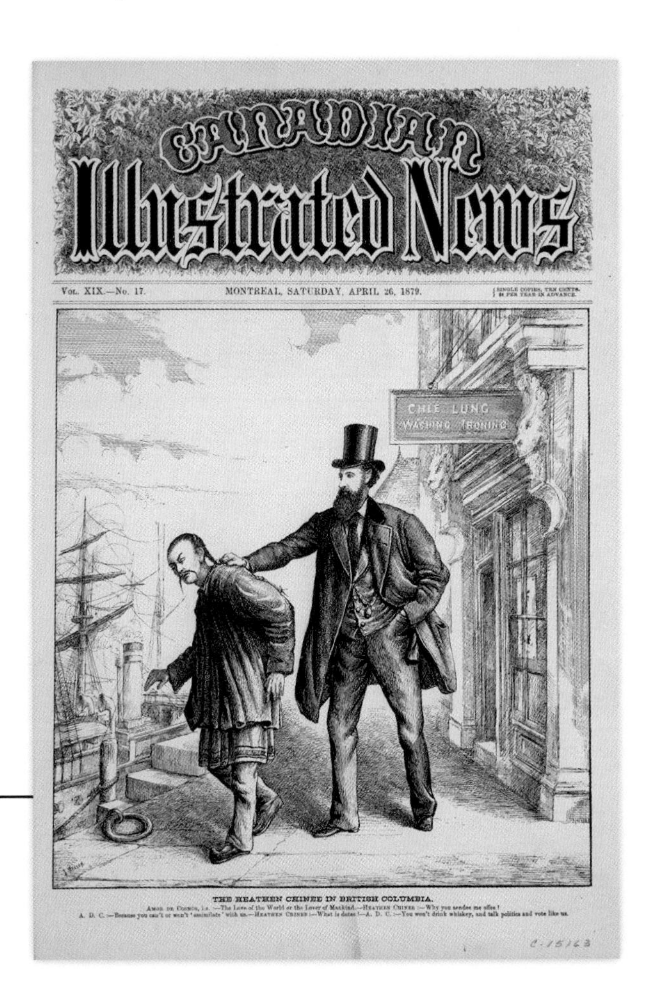

Canadian Illustrated News

Vol. XIX.—No. 17. MONTREAL, SATURDAY, APRIL 26, 1879. SINGLE COPIES, TEN CENTS. $4 PER YEAR IN ADVANCE.

THE HEATHEN CHINEE IN BRITISH COLUMBIA.

Amor de Cosmos, i.e.—The Love of the World or the Lover of Mankind.—Heathen Chinee:—Why you sendee me offee! A. D. C.:—Because you can't or won't 'assimilate' with us.—Heathen Chinee:—What is datee?—A. D. C.:—You won't drink whiskey, and talk politics and vote like us.

C-15163

The caption to this 1879 cartoon expresses the racist beliefs held by many white Canadians at the time: "You won't drink whisky, and talk politics, and vote like us."

78742
DOMINION OF CANADA
NEW C.I. 5 SERIES
IMMIGRATION BRANCH – DEPARTMENT OF THE INTERIOR
RECEIVED FROM
whose photograph is attached hereto, on the date and at the place hereunder mentioned, the sum of Five Hundred Dollars being the head tax due under the provisions of the Chinese Immigration Act.
The above mentioned party who claims to be a native of
in the of
of the age of years arrived or landed at on the day of 19
The identification in this case is C.I. No. 48746
Dated at on APR 28 1913 19
CONTROLLER OF CHINESE IMMIGRATION

(ABOVE) The Chinese workers lived in ramshackle camps alongside the dirt, noise, and mess of the railway tracks.

(RIGHT) Chinese immigrants were the only group ever required to pay a head tax. They received a certificate like this one when they did. On June 22, 2006, the Canadian government apologized to the Chinese community for the racist policy. It also offered $20,000 to anyone who had paid the head tax.

THE FIRST CHINESE IMMIGRANTS

Chinese rail workers were not the first Chinese immigrants to Canada. The first wave arrived in British Columbia in 1858, lured by the gold rush happening along the Fraser River. The first Chinese settlement grew in Barkerville a few years later, during the Cariboo Gold Rush.

The Head Tax

The same year the railway was completed—and the Chinese workers were no longer needed—the government passed the Chinese Immigration Act. This law said that every Chinese person who wanted to enter Canada had to pay a head tax, or entry tax, of $50. This was a lot of money in the 1880s—much more than most people could afford. It made it impossible for all but the wealthiest Chinese people to immigrate to Canada. The wives and children of workers already living here remained at home in China with little hope of reuniting with their families. For decades, the majority of Chinese people living in Canada were men.

The Birth of

In the late 1800s and early 1900s, most of the people living in Canada were of European descent. Many believed that Asians were inferior, and as a result Chinese immigrants faced widespread discrimination. Besides earning less than white workers doing the same jobs, they were not allowed to vote, and most landlords refused to rent to them. When Asian immigrants continued to arrive in Canada despite the head tax, anti-Asian sentiments spread and hostility grew.

Many people would have simply given up, but these were men who had survived working on the railway. They had faced back-breaking labour, landslides, explosions, hunger, and fatigue. They did not have the money to return to China, so they were determined to make the best of it in Canada.

Very quickly, the Chinese learned that if they were going to survive in a country that didn't really want them, they needed to band together and support one another with shelter, services, and even simple conversation. Many decided to make their own jobs and build their own success. This sparked the growth of Chinese neighbourhoods—or "Chinatowns"—in several cities, most notably Victoria, Vancouver, and Toronto.

These neighbourhoods were lifesavers for men who—because of the head tax—were separated from their families. In Chinatowns, the men maintained ties to their homeland and their heritage. They set up restaurants, bakeries, and grocery stores that offered familiar foods. They established Chinese newspapers and opened stores to sell imported goods, including traditional Chinese herbs and medicines. Living close together allowed Chinese immigrants to socialize, speak their own language (usually Cantonese), and practise their religions. They also founded organizations to help those who were new to the community.

Over time, most Chinatowns grew bigger and more prosperous. Today, most major Canadian cities have a Chinatown, with some cities home to several. The Greater Toronto Area (GTA) has six, with a combined population of half a million people.

This photo of a tailor was taken around 1889 in Victoria, British Columbia. Like many skilled workers, he chose to go into business for himself, making things for other Chinese immigrants.

CHINATOWNS

(ABOVE) Many Chinese immigrants started restaurants. They could serve their fellow Chinese Canadians without needing to speak English.

(RIGHT) In 1907, hostility toward Asian immigrants boiled over in Vancouver. A riot broke out and a mob of thousands stormed through the city's Chinese and Japanese neighbourhoods, smashing windows, destroying shops, and attacking people.

Italian Immigrants

When the government first began trying to attract immigrants with the offer of free land in the West, it focused on northern and eastern Europeans, like Ukrainians and Hungarians. It deliberately avoided advertising to immigrants from southern European countries, like Italy. At the time, many Canadians believed that southern Europeans were unreliable and didn't work hard—and therefore were not suitable for Canada.

A New Source of Cheap Labour

By the late 1800s, however, there was a railway to build and new industries popping up across the country. Many companies were eager for any workers they could get, no matter where they came from. The Canadian Pacific Railway had already been allowed to bring men from China, and now the owners of construction companies, sawmills, mines, and factories wanted to bring cheap labour from other countries as well.

Companies began to turn their attention to Italy. Economic conditions were bad there, and unskilled young men were willing to go just about anywhere they had a chance to earn money and make a better life. But the Italians were not English-speaking, and the Canadian government wasn't interested in recruiting them. Companies had to find their own way of attracting Italian labourers to Canada.

The *Padroni*

That's when two brothers, Vincenzo and Giovanni Veltri, stepped forward. They had first come to Canada in 1885, to work on the railway. As the demand for Italian labour began to grow, they saw a business opportunity. They set themselves up as labour agents, known as *padroni*, and worked to bring their countrymen to Canada. Soon, other Italian Canadians were following their lead. The *padroni* made money by taking fees from the employers, the steamship companies, and the workers. In return, companies got labourers, steamship companies got passengers, and Italian workers got passage to Canada and a job.

The Italian Waves

From the mines and railways of British Columbia to the farms of Manitoba and the steel mills of Nova Scotia, Italians helped build the economy of their new home. Over time, more and more came to Canada. Between 1901 and 1910, about 60,000 Italians made the long voyage across the Atlantic Ocean. Canadian cities were just then beginning to expand, and that attracted people with a whole new set of skills—bricklayers, stonemasons, shoemakers, and shopkeepers. Another even larger wave of Italian immigrants arrived between 1950 and 1970. Today, there are more than 1.3 million Canadians who claim Italian ancestry.

(TOP LEFT) By the early 1900s, Italian men were bringing over their wives and children and making Canada their permanent home. Italian neighbourhoods known as "Little Italys" began to emerge in cities.

(TOP RIGHT) Many early Italian immigrants were skilled tradespeople like this shoemaker. They brought their skills with them and started new businesses in Canada, becoming some of the country's earliest entrepreneurs.

(BOTTOM) During the construction of the Welland Canal in Ontario, in 1914, Italian labourers laid railway tracks for rail cars to move heavy loads into and out of the construction areas.

The Last, Best West

In the 1890s, Canada's approach to settling the West changed dramatically. Only a few thousand settlers had been drawn to the Prairies, and most of those were people who'd already been living in Ontario. To grow the country, populate the Prairies, and spur the spread of agriculture and other industries, the government needed to attract more newcomers from other countries.

Open Mind, Open Doors

The government that was elected in 1896 viewed the old approach of aiming mainly for British settlers as a failure. Clifford Sifton, the new minister of the interior, tackled the challenge of attracting immigrants to the Prairies with a whole new attitude. While the men who'd had the job before him believed that only immigrants from Britain, the United States, and a few parts of Europe would do, Sifton simply wanted farmers and farm workers. He cared less about where they came from than about what they would do once they arrived.

Because of Sifton's attitude, Canada began advertising the promise of the Prairies all across Europe in a campaign known as "The Last, Best West." The government opened immigration offices throughout Europe, posted agents there to recruit people, and arranged for foreign reporters to tour the Prairies so they could write glowing descriptions of what they found. The government also hired representatives to promote Canada overseas with exhibits at fairs and festivals, which presented Canada as a land of plenty—an idea that would be appealing to Europe's struggling peasant farmers.

(ABOVE) This "Girl from Canada" promoted immigration to people in Britain. She might not have convinced many to emigrate, but she certainly was attention-grabbing!

(TOP RIGHT) Canadian government officials weren't the only ones pumping money and energy into advertising the Canadian West. Many transportation companies, including railway and steamship lines, were encouraging immigration in the late 1800s and early 1900s.

(BOTTOM RIGHT) "*Lees dit!*" this poster commands. "Read this!" Many Dutch farmers must have done just that—and been persuaded to come to Manitoba. Between 1890 and 1930, about 25,000 Dutch immigrants entered Canada and headed west.

FREE FARMS FOR THE MILLION
DOMINION OF
CANADA
EXPERIMENTAL FARM, BRANDON, MANITOBA, CANADA.
EXPERIMENTAL FARM, INDIAN HEAD, NORTH WEST TERRITORY.
RED RIVER VALLEY,
Saskatchewan Valley,
THE GREAT FERTILE PLAINS
and British Columbia
CONTAIN
LARGE AREAS SUITABLE FOR GRAINS AND GRASSES
VAST MINERAL RICHES
GOLD, SILVER, IRON, COPPER, SALT, PETROLEUM, ETC., ETC.
Immense Coal Fields,
ILLIMITABLE SUPPLY OF CHEAP FUEL.
Railway from Ocean to Ocean.
SEE REPORTS OF BRITISH TENANT FARMERS WHO VISITED CANADA IN 1890.
CLIMATE THE HEALTHIEST IN THE WORLD.
CANADA HAS
5 Experimental Farms
representative of the whole settled area of the Dominion, instituted for the advancement of Agriculture.
EXPERIMENTAL FARM, NAPPAN, NOVA SCOTIA.
CENTRAL EXPERIMENTAL FARM, OTTAWA, CANADA.
EXPERIMENTAL FARM, AGASSIZ, BRITISH COLUMBIA.
FREE FARMS OF 160 ACRES
Given to every Male Adult of 18 years and over, in the great Fertile Belt of
NADIAN NORTH-WEST AND BRITISH COLUMBIA
richest in the world—easily reached by railroads. Wheat—average 30 bushels to the acre, with fair farming.
200 ACRES ARE OFFERED IN OTHER PARTS OF CANADA.
FOR CANADA,
Victoria Street, London, S.W., England.
DEPARTMENT OF THE INTERIOR, OTTAWA, CANADA.
LINE
ships
Between LIVERPOOL, BRISTOL and MONTREAL
IN SUMMER,
HALIFAX and PORTLAND, MAINE, in Winter.
FOR ALL INFORMATION, APPLY TO
FLINN, MAIN & MONTGOMERY,
24, JAMES ST., LIVERPOOL.
Managing Directors.

Lees dit!
HET BESTE TARWELAND EN WEIDELAND DER
WERELD.
64 HECTAREN IN Manitoba
en groote Noord Westen AMERIKA.
KOSTELOOS VERKRIJGBAAR LANGS DE LINIE DER
CANADIAN PACIFIC SPOORWEG
10 DAGEN VAN Holland.
BESCHRIJVINGEN, KAARTEN EN VERDERE INLICHTINGEN WORDEN KOSTELOOS VERSTREKT DOOR

Creating the Prairie Patchwork

By 1914, millions of immigrants had made their way to Canada's Prairie provinces. They included Ukrainians, Poles, Russians, Germans, Scandinavians, Hungarians, Romanians, French, and Dutch. These hard-working settlers established Canada's thriving Prairie wheat farms and other agriculture, which in turn helped spur the growth of other industries, and towns and cities. They also laid the foundations for Canada's multicultural character.

Forging Ties on the Way

Immigrants heading to the Prairies from overseas had a lot of time to get to know others making the same trip. The ocean voyage alone sometimes took a month—an unpleasantly rough thirty days, in most cases. When the travellers landed in Halifax, they still faced a seemingly endless train ride west. Most would board one of the so-called colonist cars, which were added to many trains expressly for these new settlers. Five hundred or more adults and children would spend five or six long days chugging along in these cars, their few possessions at their feet as they crowded together on bare wooden benches that converted into sleeping berths at night. To help pass the time, passengers would chat, exchange farming tips and recipes, and share dreams and fears. And so a sense of togetherness was born.

Block Settlements

Once they reached the Prairies, settlers who shared an ethnic background deliberately chose lots near one another, so they could be close to people who shared their language and culture. It was a way of feeling a bit more at home in a strange and unfamiliar land. Their block settlements quickly became small, tight-knit communities. They continued to speak their own languages, cook familiar foods, and practise traditions from their homelands, keeping their distinct culture and heritage alive. Blocks of different cultures sprang up across the Prairies, where they still flourish to this day.

Religious "Patches"

Several religious groups, including Mennonites, Doukhobors, Hutterites, and Mormons, also arrived on the Prairies with a plan to form their own communities. These groups had been persecuted for their beliefs in the countries they came from. On the Prairies, they could settle away from mainstream society and the discrimination that usually came with it. Many lived communally, sharing land, farm work, and crops. For the most part, the Canadian government allowed these groups to practise their religions and to live in their chosen ways without interference.

(**ABOVE**) These Ukrainian immigrants wait with their few possessions on a train platform. They are heading west to claim homesteads.

(**ABOVE**) In the early 1900s, there was a boom of settlers who wanted free homesteads in Canada's West. This photo shows a crowd outside the Dominion Land Office in Moose Jaw, Saskatchewan, in 1908.

(**RIGHT**) Russian Doukhobors have always believed strongly in working together and lending a helping hand. Here, a group of women work as a team to plough their shared field.

The Ukrainians

When Canada's first Ukrainian immigrants, Ivan Pylypiw and Wasyl Elenia, arrived in 1891, they embodied Clifford Sifton's vision of Canada's ideal settlers: hard-working farmers used to a harsh climate. Sifton had described the immigrant he hoped to attract as "a stalwart peasant in a sheep-skin coat, born on the soil, whose forefathers have been farmers for ten generations."

The Ukrainian Wave

Pylypiw and Elenia were the first of a wave of Ukrainian immigrants spurred on by widespread poverty in their homeland. At that time, most Ukrainian farmers didn't own the tiny plots of poor farmland they worked. They paid landlords sky-high rents and had little left afterward. The promise of free, rich farmland was hard to resist, and thousands of Ukrainian families packed their sparse belongings to start a new life on the Prairies. By 1914, about 170,000 Ukrainians had settled from Winnipeg to Edmonton, making them one of the Prairies'—and the country's—largest ethnic groups.

Strength in Numbers

When Ukrainian immigrants finally arrived on the Prairies after weeks of travelling by ship and rail, there was no time to rest. They had to get busy creating their homesteads right away. To choose their lots, the settlers would head to the homestead office and study a map of the local area. Of course, it was impossible to tell from a map what the land would actually be like.

Like most non-English-speaking immigrants, Ukrainians usually chose neighbouring lots, even if that meant some would end up with poor-quality land. Being close to relatives, friends, and fellow villagers from back home was more important than anything else.

Ukrainian homesteaders looked out for one another as they struggled to clear and farm their homesteads, survive harsh winters, and make it through lean years when crops failed. Once they had established their own homesteads, they often took in newly arrived Ukrainian families and helped them build their first Canadian homes.

(ABOVE) Ukrainian immigrants formed strong, tight-knit communities on the Prairies. This photograph from 1917 shows a group of settlers wearing their finest traditional Ukrainian clothing at a wedding.

(BOTTOM LEFT) Ukrainian children stand in front of the lean-to shelter their family first lived in when they arrived on their homestead, and then proudly pose with the tidy log house their family built to replace it.

(BELOW) These dancers are from a Ukrainian folk group in Edmonton, Alberta. These groups exist across Canada to help teach new generations of Ukrainian Canadians about their heritage.

UKRAINIAN CANADIANS TODAY

Today, more than a million people consider themselves Ukrainian Canadians. Each year, thousands enjoy the National Ukrainian Festival in Dauphin, Manitoba, the largest celebration of Ukrainian culture in North America. There, people eat traditional foods, including kolbassa (a seasoned sausage) and borscht (a beet soup), and participate in dance competitions. In communities across the country, modern Ukrainian Canadians have made a deliberate effort to maintain their traditions, including their language, foods, and cultural practices.

The Americans

Although the Canadian government had long feared a takeover of the West by the United States, it was also keen to attract American immigrants. Clifford Sifton believed that these settlers would bring money, goods, and knowledge of prairie farming, so they were sure to be successful.

In the 1890s, the government did everything it could to encourage American farmers with money to spend to make the move to the Prairies. It plastered western states with advertising campaigns and set up immigration offices to entice farmers to head north. The timing was perfect. Most of the free land offered in the United States had been claimed, and good farmland was quickly becoming expensive to buy.

Clifford Sifton's efforts worked: between 1901 and 1914, almost a million Americans made the move north. About one-third of these were European immigrants who originally landed in America but decided their chances for land were better in Canada. They included German, Icelandic, Hungarian, Dutch, and Scandinavian settlers.

American immigrants brought important technologies, including steel ploughs and barbed wire, as well as knowledge of farming techniques for dry areas. These innovations helped the agriculture industry expand across even the driest parts of the Prairies, and created the focus on wheat farming. American settlers also helped establish ranching on the Prairies.

(ABOVE) Many Americans could not afford the cost of train fare, so they journeyed to western Canada on "prairie schooners," or covered wagons, like these. The wagons were pulled by horses or oxen and covered with a tarp to protect the settlers' belongings. Everything they owned was piled inside.

Alberton apr 20/1910

KEEP THE NEGRO ACROSS THE LINE

THE WINNIPEG BOARD OF TRADE TAKES DECIDED ACTION

Not Good Settlers or Agreeable Neighbors Either

Winnipeg, Man., April 19.—The Winnipeg board of trade this evening passed a strongly worded resolution, which will be forwarded to Ottawa, condemning the admission of negroes into Canada as settlers.

It is set forth in the resolution that these new-comers are not successful farmers nor agreeable neighbors for white settlers. The board also passed a resolution similar to that of the Manufacturers' association on the proposal to amend the railway act to enable the railway commission to suspend railway tariffs or charges on appeals from patrons of the railways against which grievances are held.

Ads promoting the opportunities awaiting American farmers in the Canadian West flooded the Midwestern United States.

(LEFT) Around 1910, black farmers from Oklahoma started moving to Saskatchewan, Manitoba, and Alberta. These new Canadians were fed up with American laws that wouldn't allow them to vote, own property, or have access to education. But as this newspaper article shows, they continued to face discrimination in Canada.

Chapter 3

CLOSING THE DOORS

In the early 1900s, Canada received millions of immigrants from Europe, the United States, and Asia. Although the West was expanding and Canada's economy was booming, tensions were also rising as a result of so many newcomers.

At the time, most Canadians had British backgrounds, spoke English, and practised the Protestant faith. More and more, they began to resent immigrants who did not seem to be conforming to their idea of what it meant to be a Canadian. French Canadians started to fear that their culture and language would be swallowed up in the tide of newcomers. Aboriginal peoples continued to face discrimination and alienation.

And then came a series of tough challenges that would increase tensions even further: two world wars and a massive economic collapse called the Great Depression. Each of these challenges had an impact on immigrants—and on Canadians' ideas about "outsiders." Between 1914 and 1947, immigration to Canada came almost to a screeching halt.

BEWARE

TROOP TRAIN WRECKED
BLAME CARELESS TALK
THE WALLS
HAVE EARS
jac leonard

Controlling the Flood

In an attempt to protect Canada's "British-ness," the government introduced two immigration acts at the start of the new century—one in 1906 and another in 1910. The new acts were meant to slow immigration from eastern and central Europe, stop immigration from Asia, and boost the numbers of "preferred immigrants" from Britain and the United States.

Discouraging "Undesirables"

The immigration acts didn't come right out and say that people of certain backgrounds were not welcome, but they included requirements that made it difficult, if not impossible, for people to come to Canada from China, Japan, or India.

An example of these impossible requirements was the Continuous Passage Act, which the government passed into law in 1908. It stated that Canada would accept only immigrants who had travelled directly from their home country, with no stops along the way. Although the act didn't mention race or nationality, it was meant to keep out immigrants from non-European countries, especially Japan and India. At the time, there were no direct steamship routes from those countries to Canada.

Closing the Doors

The biggest blow to immigration came in the 1930s, with the Great Depression. Almost overnight, people across Canada found themselves struggling to find jobs, to make ends meet, and even to get enough to eat. The government responded by severely limiting immigration, in part to calm Canadians' fears that "outsiders" would take their jobs. During the 1930s, the number of immigrants dropped to one-tenth of what it had been in the 1920s.

Young women like the one pictured here were at the top of Canada's "preferred" list. A domestic servant, this ideal immigrant is happily helping to keep the farmhouse going while the men are out bringing in the harvest.

(ABOVE) The Immigration Act of 1910 stated that the government had the authority to block "immigrants belonging to any race deemed unsuited to the climate or requirements of Canada." The government used this clause to discourage African-American immigrants from the United States. Political cartoons such as this one from 1904 expressed the views of many Canadians about who made ideal immigrants.

(RIGHT) During the Great Depression, people became so desperate for work that they travelled back and forth across the country taking any jobs they could find. Groups such as the Unemployed Single Men's Association showed the government their frustration through demonstrations like this one.

The *KOMAGATA MARU*

On May 23, 1914, a ship arrived in Vancouver harbour carrying 376 would-be immigrants—and a challenge to Canada's immigration rules. The passengers aboard the ship, called the *Komagata Maru*, were Sikhs, Muslims, and Hindus from Britain's Indian colonies. They had travelled to Canada via Hong Kong, but since they were British subjects, they believed that the Continuous Passage Act should not apply to them, and that Canada should accept them as immigrants.

When the ship arrived after a month and a half at sea, those who had been looking forward to a new life in Canada were sorely disappointed. The *Komagata Maru* was not allowed to dock. Its passengers had to remain aboard the ship, which was forced to anchor offshore. Only twenty-two of the passengers—all of them former residents of Canada—were eventually allowed off.

A Sikh-Canadian businessman named Gurdit Singh (wearing the light suit) chartered the *Komagata Maru*. He wanted to challenge the Continuous Passage Act and the discriminatory attitude behind it.

Two long months passed. During that time, the *Komagata Maru*'s passengers were treated as virtual prisoners. Canadian officials denied them access to lawyers. They refused to provide food or water for them. They didn't even give the passengers a reason for their detention. The officials hoped to force the passengers to turn around before they could challenge the "continuous passage" requirement in court.

Meanwhile, a group of Indian Canadians and other supporters formed a Shore Committee to help the passengers. They provided food, hired a lawyer, and raised money for legal fees. They sent telegrams to politicians in both Canada and India, and eventually they took the case all the way to the Supreme Court of Canada.

In the end, the court ruled that the passengers could not land in Canada for a number of reasons, but mainly because they had travelled from India via Hong Kong. The ship was ordered to return to India. On July 23, 1914, the Canadian navy escorted the *Komagata Maru* out of the harbour.

The case showed that not all people were welcome in Canada, whether they were British subjects or not. Since the 1990s, South Asian groups in Canada have been asking for an apology. On May 16, 2016, Prime Minister Justin Trudeau formally apologized in the House of Commons for the *Komagata Maru* incident.

(TOP) During their two months of captivity, the passengers had to make do with the few supplies they already had aboard.

(BOTTOM) Most Canadians, in Vancouver and elsewhere, were unsympathetic to the passengers. Many turned out to watch the ship be escorted from the harbour.

TURNED AWAY: The SS *St. Louis*

On June 7, 1939, an ocean liner about two days south of Halifax radioed for permission to land at Pier 21, Canada's main centre for processing immigrants. The ship was carrying more than 900 Jewish passengers fleeing Nazi Germany and the rising violence aimed at them there. Canada denied the ship's request.

More than three weeks earlier, the ship had set sail for Cuba, and the passengers were filled with mixed emotions. They were relieved to be escaping Germany, sad about leaving behind friends and family, and optimistic about what lay ahead in Cuba. They spent the Atlantic crossing enjoying the ship as if on holiday—dancing, dining, swimming, and watching films in the cinema.

All the passengers had obtained Cuban visas. But while they were en route to the island, Cuba had a change of heart. When the ship arrived, it was not allowed to enter the harbour. For more than a week, diplomats tried to persuade Cuban officials to honour the visas and allow the passengers ashore. In the end, the ship was forced to leave.

The ship sailed north, passing close enough to Miami for the passengers to see the city in the distance. The captain, Gustav Schroeder, radioed for permission to land in the United States, but his request went unanswered.

With hope fading, Captain Schroeder continued north toward Halifax and asked for permission to dock. When government officials received the request, they refused to help. When asked how many Jewish refugees Canada should accept, one immigration official said, "None is too many."

When Canada denied entry to the passengers on the SS *St. Louis*, Captain Schroeder had no choice but to turn his ship back toward Europe. The mood on the return trip was sombre. Passengers cried or wandered the ship in silence, dreading their return to Germany.

In the end, the passengers didn't have to go back. Britain, France, Belgium, and the Netherlands agreed to take them in. Unfortunately, after the Second World War broke out in September, the Nazis eventually took control of all those countries except Britain. More than 250 of the SS *St. Louis*'s passengers were killed in concentration camps during the Holocaust.

Although Canada agreed to accept about 4,000 Jewish refugees after the war broke out, there were hundreds of thousands of Jews seeking shelter from danger. Of all democratic countries, Canada was one of those taking in the fewest Jewish refugees.

(TOP RIGHT) With no country willing to accept them, the Jewish refugees aboard the SS *St. Louis* had no choice but to return to Europe. More than 250 later died in the Holocaust.

(BOTTOM RIGHT) During the Second World War, the British government encouraged parents to send their kids away from the bombing in London and other cities. Thousands of Canadian families opened their homes to British guest children. The children returned home to Britain when the war ended.

GUEST CHILDREN

The government didn't turn down everyone's request for safe haven. Canadian families hosted almost 8,000 British children during the Second World War. Posters like this one appeared on streets throughout Britain's major cities, urging parents to send their children to safety, away from bombing campaigns and a potential German invasion.

The Gateway to Canada

Until about fifty years ago, almost all immigrants to Canada arrived by sea. The majority of ships came across the Atlantic Ocean from Europe, and they docked at ports on Canada's east coast. Halifax was one of the busiest.

In 1928, the government set up Pier 21 specifically to assess and process all the potential immigrants arriving at the port. Each day, ships docked with hundreds of passengers. After that began the nail-biting process that all new immigrants to Canada would share, no matter their country of origin or their dreams for the future. Would they be allowed to stay? Or would they be turned back?

At times, as many as 4,000 people needed processing, and that meant a lot of waiting and moving from room to room. Hundreds of weary, excited, anxious travellers sat on long wooden benches, some bouncing babies on their knees and clutching passports in their fists. Others stood while waiting for their names to be called, arms crossed or hands jammed in pockets, too nervous to sit.

When they recognized their names, the new arrivals breathed a sigh of relief and headed off to the next room, families and belongings in tow. Here there were wooden tables staffed by immigration officers who gave quick smiles and invited them to sit. Documents and immigration papers, carried possessively across thousands of kilometres, were handed over. The officers read quickly and carefully, going through the information with the tired travellers. "This is your name? This is where you were born? Where are you headed in Canada? Is all this correct?"

Many immigrants spoke no English or French, so the staff included interpreters who knew the most common languages—German, Italian, Dutch, and Russian. Once the newcomers were able to understand—and make themselves understood—there came the medical examinations. Then luggage was inspected and sorted. The whole process took hours. But what were a few more hours after the days spent crossing the ocean and the weeks or months spent preparing for the long trip in the first place?

And when the words "Landed immigrant" were stamped on a new Canadian's immigration ID card, the long wait, the exhaustion, and the stomach-churning anxiety all melted away. Here was a fresh start. Here was a welcoming Canada.

From 1928 to 1971, more than a million immigrants passed through the doors of Pier 21, the immigration station that became the so-called Gateway to Canada.

(TOP LEFT) After their long journey crossing the ocean and the hours waiting for their names to be called, some young immigrants had a hard time keeping their heads up and their eyes open.

(TOP RIGHT) Volunteer interpreters who spoke less common languages would respond promptly to a phone call from Pier 21 asking for help. Every new arrival was eventually paired up with someone who could help him or her understand the questions about to be asked.

(BOTTOM) Immigrants no longer pass through Pier 21. Today, it is a museum where visitors can learn the stories of immigrants and see their travel documents, souvenirs, and other pieces of history.

Handtekening van de houder
Signature du titulaire / Signature of bearer
(THIRD CLASS)
IDENTIFICATION
STERLING SILVER
NAAM VAN DE HOUDER
NOM DU PORTEUR / NAME OF BEARER
SIGNALEMENT
Beroep / Profession / Occupation
Woonplaats / Domicile / Residence
Nationaliteit / Nationalité / Nationality
NEDERLANDSE

Chapter 4

WELCOMING THE WORLD

In the second half of the twentieth century, Canada underwent a lot of changes that helped open the country's doors. Many started in the aftermath of the Second World War. Britain's status as a world power faded, and the idea of British superiority faded with it. Canadians began to see their country as separate from Britain. Canada's booming postwar economy gave Canadians from all backgrounds the opportunity to get ahead—and they did. All these changes made Canadians open to welcoming more immigrants from places outside Britain and western Europe.

Meanwhile, people of all nations became more connected through newspapers, radio, and television, which also changed how Canadians saw the world and their place in it. Television brought the awful reality of wars and their refugees into Canadian living rooms. Problems people faced in other parts of the world didn't seem so distant anymore, and Canadians wanted to help.

The United Nations was formed in 1945, and ideas like human rights and equal rights for all people began to spread. Humanitarianism and tolerance became entrenched values in Canada, as did multiculturalism. The government's approach to immigration shifted over the years to reflect these changes in Canadian values and attitudes. The country's doors gradually opened wider and wider, until Canada found itself welcoming the world.

A Safe Haven for Refugees

Although there have been refugees for as long as there have been wars and violent conflicts, the idea that safe and stable countries had an obligation to help these people didn't become official until 1950, when the Office of the United Nations High Commissioner for Refugees was formed. In 1951, many countries signed the UN's Convention Relating to the Status of Refugees, an agreement that defined who can be considered a refugee, what obligations host countries have toward refugees, and what rights and obligations refugees have in a host country. Canada did not sign the agreement until 1969.

Refuge for Some

Even though Canada did not originally sign the UN agreement, it did take in refugees during the 1950s and 1960s—just not as many as it could have. The government wanted to maintain control of who could come to Canada, and from where. But it faced more and more pressure throughout the 1960s from church groups, humanitarian organizations, and everyday Canadians who believed their country had an obligation to do more. In 1971, Canada welcomed some of its first non-European refugees, 228 Tibetans.

Refuge for All

It wasn't until the Immigration Act of 1976 passed that Canada officially recognized refugees as a separate class of immigrants. Just a few years later, in 1979, Canada saw the start of a wave of refugees from Vietnam, Cambodia, and other Southeast Asian countries. People were trying to escape the Vietnam War, violent dictatorships, and Communist rule. Church groups, community groups, and individual Canadians rushed forward to help the newcomers settle in, offering them food, clothing, and places to stay until they could get on their feet. Between 1979 and 1980, more than 60,000 Southeast Asian refugees found a safe haven in Canada.

In the decades since, Canada has opened its doors to 10,000 to 20,000 refugees each year. They have come from more than 140 countries in every part of the world, including eastern Europe, Latin America, Africa, and the Middle East.

(BOTTOM LEFT) These families arrived from Rome on Christmas Eve 1959. They were part of Canada's efforts during the United Nations' World Refugee Year. The children received Christmas presents donated by schoolchildren in Guelph, Ontario.

(TOP AND ABOVE) In 1972, Ugandan dictator Idi Amin gave all Asian people in the African country ninety days to leave. Between September and November of that year, Canada accepted more than 6,000 Ugandan refugees.

A HUNGARIAN

After the Second World War ended, the Soviet Union took control of Hungary. The Communist government limited people's freedoms and controlled everything from the economy to schools to the media. It also banned religion. Hungarians were not happy with the changes.

In 1956, that unhappiness erupted into a revolution. University students and ordinary Hungarians took to the streets. Many were armed only with kitchen utensils and other makeshift weapons. They wanted to force the Soviets from the country. The Russians responded by sending in tanks to crush the rebellion. Across Hungary, roughly 2,500 people were killed. Another 250,000 fled the country between late 1956 and early 1957. Canada admitted about 37,000 Hungarian refugees. This is the story of one.

Tony Kuzak was a student protesting at the Forest Engineering University in the city of Sopron when the tanks rolled in. "It happened on November 4, 1956," he remembers. "We tried to defend Sopron from the approaching Soviet tanks, but we failed. Many of the students and professors left to avoid the cruelties expected from the Russians. We fled to Austria, [and] most of us did not take anything with us. I didn't even have an overcoat." In total, the dean of the university, about two dozen professors, and more than 300 students managed to escape.

In Austria, the dean approached a few professors to see if there was some way the students could continue their studies. With the help of the Austrian government, he collected all the students and teachers together in one refugee camp, and then he began writing to foreign governments, looking for a new home.

"Canada's response was the most generous," Kuzak recalls. The government "agreed to adopt the staff and students of our 200-year-old university [and fold it] into the University of British Columbia as a special faculty of forestry. The opportunities in British Columbia for foresters seemed the best in the whole world."

In January 1957, the Canadian government arranged for the students and faculty members to travel to Canada. They spent the next several months learning English. Then, in September, their classes began again. Every year, students graduated and spread across Canada. Most of them successfully found work in the forestry industry.

"With the Hungarian Revolution still fresh in our memories," Kuzak says, "we felt responsible for the honour of Hungary. Because of this, despite language, social, and emotional difficulties, we carried on with our lectures and studying." He was rewarded for all his hard work with a teaching position at UBC, and he soon settled down to start a family. Tony Kuzak says, "It is obvious to me that Canada is the greatest country in the whole world."

(RIGHT) In Budapest, Hungary, Canadian embassy officials rented out a dance hall so they would be able to process would-be refugees quickly and get them on their way to Canada.

REFUGEE'S Story

(RIGHT) Although it lasted just eleven days, the Hungarian Revolution—a spontaneous uprising of ordinary citizens—changed the lives of hundreds of thousands of people forever.

(LEFT) Many Hungarian refugees, like these, first came to Canada after the collapse of the Austro-Hungarian Empire at the end of the First World War. Others soon followed—to escape the Second World War and its aftermath, and then in the wake of the revolution. Today, there are about 250,000 Canadians of Hungarian descent.

American Draft Dodgers

During the 1950s, tensions rose between the world's two new superpowers: the Soviet Union and the United States. The world found itself caught up in a Cold War, with Western countries like Canada and Britain siding with the United States against the Soviet Union. The Soviets and the Americans tried to extend their influence over more and more countries. Each was afraid that the other would take control of the world.

The Vietnam War

In the mid-1950s, Vietnam had been divided in two. The Soviets backed the north, while the Americans backed the south. The Americans feared that if South Vietnam fell to the Communists, other Asian nations would follow, like "a row of dominoes." Soon, their support sucked them into a full-fledged war. By 1965, there were nearly 60,000 US troops in Vietnam.

Support for the War Falters

At first, many Americans volunteered to fight. But as more and more troops were needed, voluntary enlistment wasn't enough. Soon, young people were being drafted, or recruited, for obligatory military service. At the same time, public opinion started to turn against the war. Thousands of US soldiers were dying in a conflict that many Americans felt had nothing to do with them. With news reports bringing the reality of war into millions of homes every night, opposition grew.

Dodging the Draft

Many draftees did not wish to fight, but those who refused faced jail time. So thousands decided to "dodge" the draft and head north to Canada. Canada was close by, uninvolved in the war, and not legally obliged to return draft dodgers to the United States. Between 1964 and 1977, 50,000 to 125,000 Americans slipped across the border, most of them probably intending to stay only as long as the war lasted. But during those years, many found themselves compatible with Canadian society and its values. Even after President Jimmy Carter pardoned the draft dodgers in 1977, clearing the way for them to return to the United States, most chose to stay. They had become Canadians.

(LEFT) Protestors appeared at the United States' pavilion at the Montreal Expo in 1967. The anti-war movement deeply divided the nation. To this day, Americans will still argue passionately for and against the Vietnam War.

(ABOVE) A group of war objectors, including American draft dodgers, gathered outside Toronto's City Hall in 1967 to protest the war. Those who came to Canada entered the country as landed immigrants. They became the largest, best-educated group of immigrants Canada had ever received.

IN FOREIGN TERRITORY

John Hagan was a draft dodger who left his home in Illinois for Edmonton in 1969. "Being born in a country is a different experience than becoming part of one," he explains. "Our new Canadian surroundings were a welcome alternative to military service in war-torn Vietnamese villages and jungles. Nevertheless [my fellow draft dodgers and I] were in foreign territory. I will always remember my father warning in a departing phone call that this was the worst mistake I could ever make," he says. But Hagan never regretted it—and clearly most other draft dodgers didn't either. About three-quarters of the Americans who found refuge in Canada never returned to live in the United States again.

Afghan Refugees

Afghanistan is a country with a long and tumultuous history. Tribes there have warred against each other for centuries, and other nations have invaded time and again. After two bloody internal revolts, the Soviet Union took over the vulnerable country in 1979. But conflict continued as the Soviets and their Afghan allies warred against opposition groups funded by the United States, Pakistan, and Saudi Arabia. By the time the Soviets withdrew from Afghanistan in 1989, as many as 1 million people had been killed.

No Break from Chaos

After the Soviets left, years of civil war followed. Then, in 1994, the Taliban, a radical Islamist political group, began to take over the country. The Taliban regime engaged in large-scale human-rights violations, and most nations refused to recognize it as a legitimate government. In 2001, the United States and its allies, including Canada, launched a war against the Taliban. Although that war officially ended in 2014, the Taliban has since resurfaced and has been taking over parts of Afghanistan.

A Refugee Crisis

Since 1979, more than half of Afghanistan's 16 million citizens have vanished. Thousands were killed or injured, but many simply fled the country. The endless conflict created millions of refugees over the decades, as people left Afghanistan hoping to find safety. Millions ended up in neighbouring countries.

Over the past thirty years, thousands of Afghan refugees made their way to Canada, where they settled mainly in cities. Here, they recreated some of the feel of their homeland in neighbourhoods known as "Little Kabuls." Ethnic restaurants and shops dot the streets, and in the local parks children fly colourful kites, a popular Afghan pastime.

THE SYRIAN REFUGEE CRISIS

Starting in 2010, a series of uprisings known as the Arab Spring spread throughout the Arab world, including many countries in the Middle East. People protested and overthrew their corrupt governments. In 2011, the protests spread to Syria as people demanded that the president, dictator Bashar al-Assad, step down. Assad responded with violence. Civil war erupted and the country fell into chaos. Since then, more than 400,000 Syrians have been killed, and more than half of all Syrians have been pushed from their war-torn towns and cities. Millions live in refugee camps in neighbouring countries. In 2015, the crisis finally gained the world's attention. During that year, thousands of Syrian refugees drowned while trying to make their way to Europe in overcrowded, unsafe boats. Shocked into action, Canadians wanted to help. By 2016, the government, community groups, churches, and other organizations arranged for more than 26,000 Syrian refugees to come to Canada.

(TOP) Although many of the people who were displaced in the Afghanistan War (2001–14) have returned home, more than a million Afghans still remain in refugee camps just outside their country's borders.

(ABOVE LEFT) Canadian soldiers fought in Afghanistan from 2001 to 2012. They provided military support, built schools, drilled wells, and delivered aid to people in need. This little boy flies a kite given to him by Canadian soldiers.

(RIGHT) When they landed at Toronto's Pearson International Airport, Syrian refugees received warm winter clothes as well as Canada culture kits, which included children's books and a copy of the *Canadian Charter of Rights and Freedoms*.

The Changing Face of Canada

Today, 20 percent of Canadians—one in five—were born in another country. That's the highest percentage in seventy-five years. With so many people coming from so many different countries and cultures, Canada has been changing over the past few decades. What it means to be "Canadian" has changed too.

The World Is Here

By the end of the 1980s, more than half of all immigrants came from countries outside of Europe, and that still holds true today. Since the early 2000s, the top places of origin—the countries immigrants come from—have been India, China, the Philippines, Pakistan, the United States, Iran, and the United Kingdom.

More Urban and Ethnic

Over the past few decades, most newcomers settled in cities, making Canada more urban than rural. (That means the majority of Canadians now live in cities.) Neighbourhoods with distinct ethnic characteristics popped up in Montreal, Toronto, Vancouver, and other cities across the country.

New immigrants are drawn to cities for a number of reasons, including jobs, family, and a sense of belonging. People who don't speak much English or French can get by in these neighbourhoods, where residents still speak in their mother tongues. They can find comfort in the familiar, with shops, restaurants, and other businesses offering a bit of "home" in Canada.

A Canadian Identity?

A country's identity is its unique culture and characteristics—what makes it stand out from other countries. Some people believe that Canada does not have a distinct identity of its own because people from so many different cultures live here. Others argue that its multicultural character is part of its identity. Canada, they believe, is a nation of nations. They claim that the very things it takes to make a country work with so many diverse groups living together are what gives Canada its identity: regard for human rights, acceptance of differences, and respect for equality.

(TOP RIGHT) In 1966, almost all immigrants to Canada were from Europe. By 1970, half were from other parts of the world, including the Caribbean, Hong Kong, India, and the Philippines.

(BELOW) In Quebec, Canadians of Caribbean descent celebrate their heritage every year at Carifiesta.

(**RIGHT**) Making and signing an oath of citizenship is part of the Canadian citizenship ceremony. After they make the oath, new citizens receive a citizenship certificate.

BECOMING CITIZENS

Immigrants who settle in Canada are called permanent residents. In the past, they were called landed immigrants. Permanent residents can apply to become citizens after four years. Citizens have the right to vote, get elected, join the military, and obtain a Canadian passport. This family celebrates becoming citizens after a ceremony in London, Ontario.

Chinese Immigrants

Throughout their long history in Canada, Chinese immigrants have overcome many obstacles, including official discrimination. Until the mid-1900s, the government made them unwelcome in many ways, most notably through the Chinese Exclusion Act, which passed in 1923. This law made it impossible for anyone to come to Canada from China. It was finally repealed in 1947, when Chinese Canadians also gained the right to vote, but other laws still limited how many relatives Chinese Canadians were allowed to sponsor.

When these unfair restrictions were lifted in 1967, Chinese immigrants began arriving in large numbers. Today, China is one of the top three countries of immigrants to Canada. With a population of 1.5 million, Chinese Canadians are the third-largest ethnic group in this country after English and French Canadians, and languages in the Chinese family (Mandarin, Cantonese, Taiwanese) are the third most commonly spoken.

Then and Now

Today, immigrants from China are highly educated, and many are wealthy before they arrive in Canada. Many Chinese Canadians have high-paying professional careers as lawyers, doctors, and pharmacists, which is a big change from the past, when laws kept Chinese Canadians from working in such professions.

Every year, Chinese communities across Canada host New Year festivals and parades like this one in Vancouver. They feature traditional lion dances, martial arts performances, and more, and they attract thousands of spectators.

(**TOP**) In the past, most Canadians shunned Chinatowns. Today, they are vital attractions—places where people of all backgrounds dine and shop. Victoria's Chinatown is famous for its Gates of Harmonious Interest and the world's narrowest street, Fan Tan Alley.

(**LEFT**) Despite the obstacles and discrimination Chinese people faced in Canada, soldiers such as these still proudly served their country in the Second World War.

Chinese Canadians

Today's Chinese Canadian community includes both descendants of the early immigrants and new arrivals, so it's not surprising that it is a mix of old and new traditions and values. Descendants of early immigrants pass on to their children the language and traditions of their ancestral home, and they share stories with them too—stories of their grandparents' and great-grandparents' journey to Canada, of their struggles to earn a living and carve out a place for themselves in an unfamiliar land. They have also established associations to promote their culture and strengthen their business and professional ties. Many of these groups also help recent immigrants from China adjust to their new lives. Most Chinese immigrants settle in big cities, especially Vancouver and Toronto. Combined, those two cities are home to 70 percent of Canada's Chinese community.

Chapter 5

THE CANADIAN KALEIDOSCOPE

From sea to sea, Canada today is a country that has been shaped by its First Peoples and immigrants. By allowing new arrivals to hold on to their heritage, Canada has evolved from a country with three founding peoples into a diverse, multicultural nation. Every group of immigrants has contributed in some way to Canada's vibrant character.

Many people describe Canada as a mosaic—a beautiful picture made up of countless individual pieces. Because each successive wave of immigrants adds to, and changes, the pieces in the mosaic, others think of Canada as a kaleidoscope, with constantly changing patterns. The Canada we see today is very different from the Canada of 1867 or the Canada of 1947, and the kaleidoscope will no doubt create a beautiful and different new pattern in the future as people continue to arrive in Canada from around the world.

A World of Cultures

In 1971, Prime Minister Pierre Trudeau recognized an important factor that makes Canada special when he announced that the country would be the first in the world to become officially multicultural.

The government of Prime Minister Brian Mulroney then passed the Canadian Multiculturalism Act in 1988. It gives all Canadians the freedom to preserve and share their culture, and guarantees their right to take part in society, no matter what their background is.

Thousands of cultural festivals, parades, and celebrations happen across the country every year. They are times when Canadians proudly share in and embrace one another's traditional foods, music, dancing, and costumes.

Multiculturalism makes it easier for newcomers to maintain their heritage, even as they become part of Canadian society. By encouraging Canadians to respect one another's differences, multiculturalism has helped create a society where people of all backgrounds and religions live peacefully.

(ABOVE) Every August, thousands of people of Icelandic descent gather in Gimli, Manitoba, to celebrate *Islendingadagurinn* (the Day of the Icelanders).

(ABOVE) Italian Canadians have a long and proud history in Canada, and their culture is present in many communities across the country. Café culture is common in many Italian neighbourhoods, where people gather at restaurants, cafés, pool halls, and social clubs. It's standing room only as these soccer fans root for Italy in a World Cup soccer match.

(LEFT) The Toronto Caribbean Carnival (Caribana) began in 1967 as a celebration of Caribbean culture. It was organized by members of the Caribbean community as part of Canada's centennial celebrations. Held every summer, it draws more than a million visitors to a variety of events, including masquerades, dances, steel-band street parties, and a massive parade.

A World of Religions

Along with their cultures and languages, Canada's immigrants have brought their religious beliefs as well. The Charter of Rights and Freedoms protects everyone's right to practise his or her faith freely in Canada, and the country has a long history of tolerance for different religions.

It started with the Quebec Act in 1774, in which Britain guaranteed French Canadians the right to continue practising Roman Catholicism in British North America, which was Protestant. In the 1800s, the government allowed people of various faiths, including Mennonites, Hutterites, Jews, and Mormons, to freely practise their religion as a way of making Canada attractive to immigrants. In the late 1900s, religious freedom was protected as a basic human right, and today Canadians continue to practise a variety of faiths.

(BELOW LEFT) These Tamil Canadians practise their Hindu faith at the Thiru Murugan Temple in Montreal.

(BELOW MIDDLE) Founded in 1856, Holy Blossom Temple in Toronto has the oldest Jewish congregation in the city. It has more than 6,500 members.

(BELOW RIGHT) Founded in 1973, the Cham Shan Temple is Toronto's oldest Chinese Buddhist temple. It is also one of the largest. At times, tens of thousands of Buddhists line up to make offerings and light incense.

(RIGHT) These students attend an Islamic school in Fort McMurray, Alberta. They are taught the Alberta curriculum from an Islamic perspective, which means their religion helps shape their lessons as well as the culture in their school.

(BELOW) Notre-Dame des Victoires, a Catholic church in Quebec City, is one of the oldest buildings in Canada still in use. It was built in 1688 on the site of Samuel de Champlain's Habitation de Québec.

CANADA'S RELIGIONS

- More than two-thirds of Canadians are Christian, making Christianity the most common faith. Within it, Roman Catholics are the largest group—almost 13 million Canadians are Roman Catholic. Two million belong to the United Church, and more than 1.6 million are Anglican.
- More than 1 million Muslims call Canada home.
- Almost 400,000 Canadians are Jewish.
- More than 300,000 Canadians are Buddhist.
- Almost 300,000 Canadians are Hindu.

A World in a City

Toronto is Canada's biggest city. It's also one of the most multicultural cities in the world. Half the people living in the city were born outside of Canada, and its residents represent more than 200 different ethnic backgrounds. A walk through its busy neighbourhoods offers the sights, sounds, and scents of India, Korea, Italy, China, Portugal, and Greece, among many other countries. It's like having the whole world reinvented on a bustling Canadian street!

After the Canadian government introduced a more liberal immigration policy in 1967, a great number of Koreans moved to this country. Many now work and shop in Toronto's Korea Town. Here, travel agencies, bakeries, acupuncture clinics, gift shops, Internet cafés, and grocery stores cater to the Korean community—and everyone else as well!

(**TOP LEFT**) This photo was taken at Toronto's downtown Chinatown, located around Dundas Street and Spadina Avenue. The neighbourhood shops sell barbecued pork, steamed buns, duck, and bok choy, among other foods. The many restaurants offer authentic Mandarin, Hunan, Szechuan, and Cantonese cuisine—with out-of-this-country flavours.

(**TOP RIGHT**) Waves of Greek immigrants came to Toronto after the Second World War. Many settled along Danforth Avenue, in the east end of the city. Stroll the street in summer and you'll see blue-and-white Greek flags hanging from windows, smell the moussaka and souvlaki cooking in restaurant kitchens, and hear Greek folk music being played on outdoor patios.

(**BOTTOM RIGHT**) When an Indian woman wants to shop for a sari or a brightly coloured scarf, she likely heads for Little India, home to the Gerrard India Bazaar. Here, she can find traditional clothing, pick up Indian groceries, and sip on some sugar-cane juice for a few minutes while she listens to the soundtrack of the latest Bollywood movie.

A WORLD of VOICES

Every day, people from countries around the world make Canada their home. Over the last few decades, Canadian immigrants have come primarily from these ten countries: China, India, Pakistan, the Philippines, South Korea, the United States, Iran, Romania, the United Kingdom, and Sri Lanka. Some new immigrants have been pushed from their own countries by circumstances there, while others have been pulled toward Canada by what they hope to find here. How does it feel to begin again somewhere new?

"I'm originally from Iran. I wanted to experience a new place, and to explore, see, and feel for myself the things that I had heard about. I'm a civil engineer. Unlike many immigrants, I was lucky enough to be able to find a job here and work in my profession. I live in Toronto, and Iranians have a big community here, so I don't miss Iran too much. I do my shopping in Iranian stores, and even my barber is an Iranian! I really like that many different people from different origins and different beliefs, cultures, and religions live peacefully together. I still feel connected to Iran, but now I am an Iranian Canadian." —Mohammed Aman

"I am originally from Romania. Leaving home was a difficult experience. It was hard to say goodbye to a life I knew so well, even though there was an adventure waiting at the other end. But this experience has helped me understand more about myself, my real strengths. I would have never known my limits if I had not chosen to come." —Manuela Stefan

"I moved to Canada from Saudi Arabia to get a better education and a better future. The hardest thing about moving here to Canada is leaving behind all my friends and cousins and all the good memories and my childhood. To this day I still miss my country and I can't forget all the fun I had. The best part of moving to Canada is meeting my cousins that I've never seen before and making new friends." —Nada Johar

"I am from India. I was very excited to see this country. I knew it had different people and a modern lifestyle that I could learn about only on television and from reading books. But I felt an emptiness as the day of moving came near. I was very sad to leave my dear grandparents and friends. I wondered, Will I feel out of place? Will I have any friends? It took me two or three months to get used to being here. My school friends and teachers helped me a lot. I feel Canada is a wonderful place. I am enjoying all the changes. But sometimes it is difficult too." —Elattuvalappil Parvathy

"I am from a poor place called Nepal. I love my country; it's my pride. It has a lots of amazing scenes, like mountain views. My father lived here before so he moved us here to make our life comfortable and to give us opportunities for success. I wasn't ready to leave Nepal because of my friends and my beloved grandma. The best part of moving to Canada is that I am free. Ever since I was young, I was taught not to be selfish because my religion is Buddhist. My leader taught me to "help if you can, but if you can't then don't hurt someone." I am happy to immigrate to Canada because it is a peaceful country. To be an immigrant to Canada is to be blessed. People here are respectful, sweet, and understandable. I respect the people and government of Canada. I want to help the country in the future if I can. Peace." —Ngawang Gyamtso

"I was born in Korea and lived there until I was four years old. I also lived in Hong Kong for about eight years before we moved to Toronto. I was very happy about the new house I was going to live in. I felt excited about moving to a new country and having new friends. But at the same time, I felt sad about leaving Hong Kong and my old friends. I think Canada is a great place to live. Everybody is very nice and comforting. I love it when it's winter here, but sometimes it gets too cold." —Jinoo Muther

"I came to Canada with my husband from Guangzhou, in China. In general, we had a good life there. We had our own apartment, and no worries about how to make a living. But we wanted to live in a country with clean air, not much pollution, rich natural resources, no heavy traffic jams, big space. And we wanted a country that could give us more fairness, more equality. Because we cannot communicate in English as fluently as we can in Chinese, we cannot get the same jobs as we had in China. However, we accept this change. We now have a Canadian-born daughter who will get the benefit from the education system here, and we hope she will have a much better future than us." —Rena Yang

"I was born in Sri Lanka. I am Tamil. I left my country because government forces were suppressing the Tamil people. Innocent people were being killed. Even though I love my country, I had to leave. This is a beautiful country, and I have found freedom here. Canada supports human rights. It is the best country in the world."
—Ghanesh Sinnappu

SEARS
NESTEKJÆRLIGHET ER REALPOLITIKK
FRIDTJOF NANSEN
1206

Conclusion

OUR PAST IS PRESENT

Everything in Canada's immigration history has helped make it the country it is today. Canada's founding peoples—Aboriginal peoples, French, and British—laid the foundations for this country. Without the help of Aboriginal peoples, early European settlers would not have survived long enough to establish the colonies that grew into Confederation. Those early French and British settlers established the systems of law and governance that Canada continues to follow today, and French and English became the country's two official languages.

As Canada grew, immigrants from Asia and eastern Europe helped build the nation and planted the roots of its multicultural society. From the isolation that created Chinatowns and Prairie block settlements grew the diversity of cultures, religions, languages, and perspectives that make up Canadian society today.

When immigrants poured in from around the globe in the late 1900s, they added their cultures, languages, and religions to the mix. They contributed to the economy and helped Canada shine on the world stage through films, books, music, sports, and scientific and medical discoveries.

Looking at Canada today, it can be tempting to think that it has always welcomed people from everywhere. But as you've read in this book, Canadians have reacted to immigration in different ways over the course of their country's history. At times, they've embraced the idea of opening the doors to newcomers to build their nation, grow their population, or strengthen their economy. At other times, they've practically barred the way.

It's important to celebrate all the times Canada opened its doors and to remember all the times it didn't—or did so grudgingly. And it's vital to acknowledge that the prejudice that led to centuries of harm to the very people who lived here first, the Aboriginal peoples, and to isolation and hardships for many immigrants and refugees, has not necessarily disappeared. Canada is getting better at recognizing past successes and failures. It is working towards becoming a nation that not only embraces the ideas of multiculturalism and inclusion but puts them into action. It's this very goal that led Canada to throw open its doors to thousands of Syrian refugees in 2015 and 2016 with the sincere greeting: "Welcome to Canada!"

Timeline

1497–2016 World Events and Canadian Immigration

World Events

1497–98
John Cabot makes two voyages from Bristol, England, to fishing grounds near Newfoundland.

1535
The name Canada is used for the first time.

1620
English settlers come to Massachusetts aboard the ship the *Mayflower*.

1670
The Hudson's Bay Company is given fur-trading rights to all lands draining into Hudson Bay.

1763
France gives up all its colonies in North America except St-Pierre and Miquelon and Louisiana.

1775–83
The Thirteen Colonies fight the American Revolution to gain their independence from Britain.

1834
Slavery is outlawed throughout the British Empire. American slaves journey to freedom on the Underground Railroad.

Canadian Immigration

1608
Samuel de Champlain founds a permanent French colony at Quebec.

1663–65
France's King Louis XIV sends troops, an administrator, and settlers to New France.

1755
British soldiers expel the Acadians from Nova Scotia.

1783–84
United Empire Loyalists make their way to Nova Scotia, Quebec, and what would become New Brunswick and Ontario.

The Great Famine kills almost a million people in Ireland.

1845–50

1847
Thousands of Irish immigrants cross the sea to Canada on rickety "coffin ships."

1872
The government passes the Dominion Lands Act to try to attract immigrants to the Prairies.

1875–85
The building of the Canadian Pacific Railroad attracts thousands of Chinese workers.

1885
The Chinese Immigration Act is passed. A head tax on Chinese immigrants is set at $50.

1891–1914
Approximately 170,000 Ukrainian immigrants come to Canada.

Gold is discovered in the Klondike.

1896

1896
Tens of thousands of people, mostly from the U.S. rush to Canada's north hoping to strike it rich.

1906
Canada passes its first official Immigration Act.

1910
The second Immigration Act is passed.

The First World War draws Britain and its colonies, including Canada, into war.

1914–1918

1923
The Chinese Immigration Act (also called the Chinese Exclusion Act) is passed. With few exceptions, it prevents "any immigrant of any Asiatic race" from coming to Canada.

Timeline (continued...)

World Events

The stock market crash marks the beginning of the Great Depression.
1929

The Second World War draws Britain and its allies into war with Germany, Italy, and Japan.
1939–1945

The Hungarian Revolution creates more than 200,000 Hungarian refugees.
1956

Canadian Immigration

1931–41
During this decade, immigration plunges. Only 140,000 immigrants arrive during these ten years. During the previous decade, more than a million arrived.

1947
Canada adopts the Canadian Citizenship Act. This act confers citizenship on both native-born and naturalized Canadians for the first time.

1952
The third Immigration Act is passed. It focuses mainly on who should be refused entry to Canada. Reasons for refusal include nationality, ethnic group, "peculiar customs," and homosexuality.

1956–57
More than 37,000 Hungarian refugees are admitted to Canada.

1959
The United Nations launches the World Refugee Year and works to resettle 110,000 refugees still in camps since the Second World War ended in 1945.

1959
Canada removes age and job restrictions from refugees and allows private sponsorship.

1960
The Canadian Bill of Rights is introduced.

1962
Canada adopts new immigration regulations that remove most of the old laws' discriminatory restrictions.

1967
The points system is introduced, removing any grounds for discrimination based on race or nationality.

1968
The Soviet Union invades Czechoslovakia.

1968–69
More than 10,000 Czech refugees enter Canada.

1969
The United States begins a draft lottery to recruit soldiers for the war in Vietnam. Resistance to the draft grows.

1971–72
Canada receives more immigrants from the United States than from any other country as young men dodge the draft.

1972
Canada celebrates the arrival of its 10 millionth immigrant since Confederation.

1972
Uganda announces that all Asian Ugandans will be forced to leave the country. They have less than three months to prepare.

1972
Canada admits more than 7,000 Asian Ugandan refugees.

Timeline (continued...)

World Events

1986
The UN awards the Nansen Refugee Award to Canadians in "recognition of their major and sustained contribution to the cause of refugees."

1998
Conflict erupts in the Kosovo region of southern Yugoslavia, creating a refugee crisis.

2003–11
The Iraq War creates more than a million refugees.

Canadian Immigration

1976
A new immigration act focuses on family reunification and the fulfilment of Canada's economic and cultural needs.

1979–80
Canada welcomes 60,000 refugees from Vietnam, Laos, and Cambodia.

1980s–90s
About 700,000 Chinese businesspeople immigrate to Canada under the new business class of immigration. They invest billions of dollars.

1998
By 1999, Canada admits more than 5,000 Kosovar refugees.

2001
Canada passes the Immigration and Refugee Protection Act. It places greater emphasis on a refugee's need for protection and less on the ability to resettle in Canada.

Revolutions known collectively as the Arab Spring lead to instability and ongoing violence in many Middle Eastern countries, including Libya, Syria, and Iraq.

2010

The Syrian Civil War starts, sparked by an uprising during the Arab Spring. By 2015, the UN registers more than 4 million refugees. It is the biggest global crisis since the Second World War.

2012–

2011–15

By 2015, Canada admits more than 22,000 Iraqi refugees.

2012–16

By 2015, Canada admits more than 6,000 Syrian refugees. It commits to bringing 25,000 more as quickly as possible. By early 2016, more than 26,000 Syrian refugees arrive in Canada.

Canada's Immigration Laws

Looking back at Canada's immigration laws over time, you can see how the country's attitude toward newcomers has changed. Throughout Canada's history, its immigration laws have been set up to boost the economy. Only in the past few decades have other considerations, like reuniting families or helping people escape war or violence, become important. Canada's immigration history also has instances of open discrimination. That's something most Canadians today find shocking.

Immigration Act, 1869

Canada's first immigration law focused mostly on protecting immigrants during their journey to Canada and after they arrived. It did not have many limitations on who could or could not come here.

The Chinese Immigration Act, 1885

This law was the first in Canada's history that excluded a specific group of people from immigrating based on their ethnicity. It called for a head tax of $50 on every Chinese person who came to Canada. In 1900, the government increased the head tax to $100 per person, and then $500 per person.

Immigration Act, 1906

This law banned many groups of people from coming to Canada, including those with epilepsy, mental illness, physical impairments, and contagious diseases. It also banned anyone who was likely to depend on the government for food, shelter, and income.

Immigration Act, 1910

This law expanded on the list of banned groups in the 1906 act and gave the government even more power to deport immigrants, or send them back to their home country. Any immigrants the government felt were "unsuited to the climate or requirements of Canada" could be blocked.

Immigration Act Amendment, 1919

At the end of the First World War, the government passed a new immigration law that addressed Canadians' worries about enemy aliens. People from countries Canada fought against in the war were banned from immigrating. The law also gave the government the power to ban immigrants based on their nationality, race, occupation, or class. People could also be barred because of "peculiar customs, habits, modes of life and methods of holding property."

Chinese Immigration Act, 1923

The act made it even more difficult for Chinese people to immigrate to Canada. Only government representatives, merchants, Canadian-born children who left and wanted to return, and students coming to attend college or university were allowed in.

Immigration Act, 1952

This act did not change much from the Immigration Act of 1910, which it replaced. Mostly, it set up a system the government could use to create new immigration regulations and gave the minister in charge of citizenship and immigration even more power to decide who could and could not come to Canada.

Immigration Regulations, 1962

These regulations were not a new immigration act, but they did make changes to the law that was in place. These included removing a person's race or ethnicity as a basis for deciding whether he or she could immigrate to Canada. Instead, an immigrant was evaluated based on his or her skills. The regulations also set up a new program that allowed Canadians to sponsor their relatives.

Immigration Regulations, 1967

Under these regulations, potential immigrants were awarded points in different categories, including their education, work skills, age, and chances of finding a job in Canada.

Immigration Act, 1976

This was the first law that actually described Canada's goals for immigration: to strengthen the economy, culture, population, and society; to reunite families; and to meet commitments to refugees. It also defined refugees as a separate class of immigrants, with their own criteria.

Immigration and Refugee Protection Act, 2001

This act replaced the law from 1976. It removed the goal relating to immigration and Canada's population and added that the country's goal to strengthen its culture through immigration should respect Canada's "multicultural" character.

Strengthening Canadian Citizenship Act, 2014

This law made changes to the Immigration Act. Some of the changes increased requirements immigrants had to meet before becoming citizens. Others gave the government the power to revoke, or take away, Canadian citizenship from dual citizens, or people who have citizenship in more than one country. Dual citizens could lose their Canadian citizenship if they were convicted of terrorism, treason, or spying. These changes were very controversial. In 2016, the government repealed, or changed back, many parts of the act.

Canada's Immigration Statistics

Over the course of Canada's history, there have been distinct trends in immigration. Canada started keeping track of the number of immigrants it received and where they came from when it began the regular census in 1871. The graphs below show how many people came to Canada during certain decades and where they came from. You can see certain trends emerge over time.

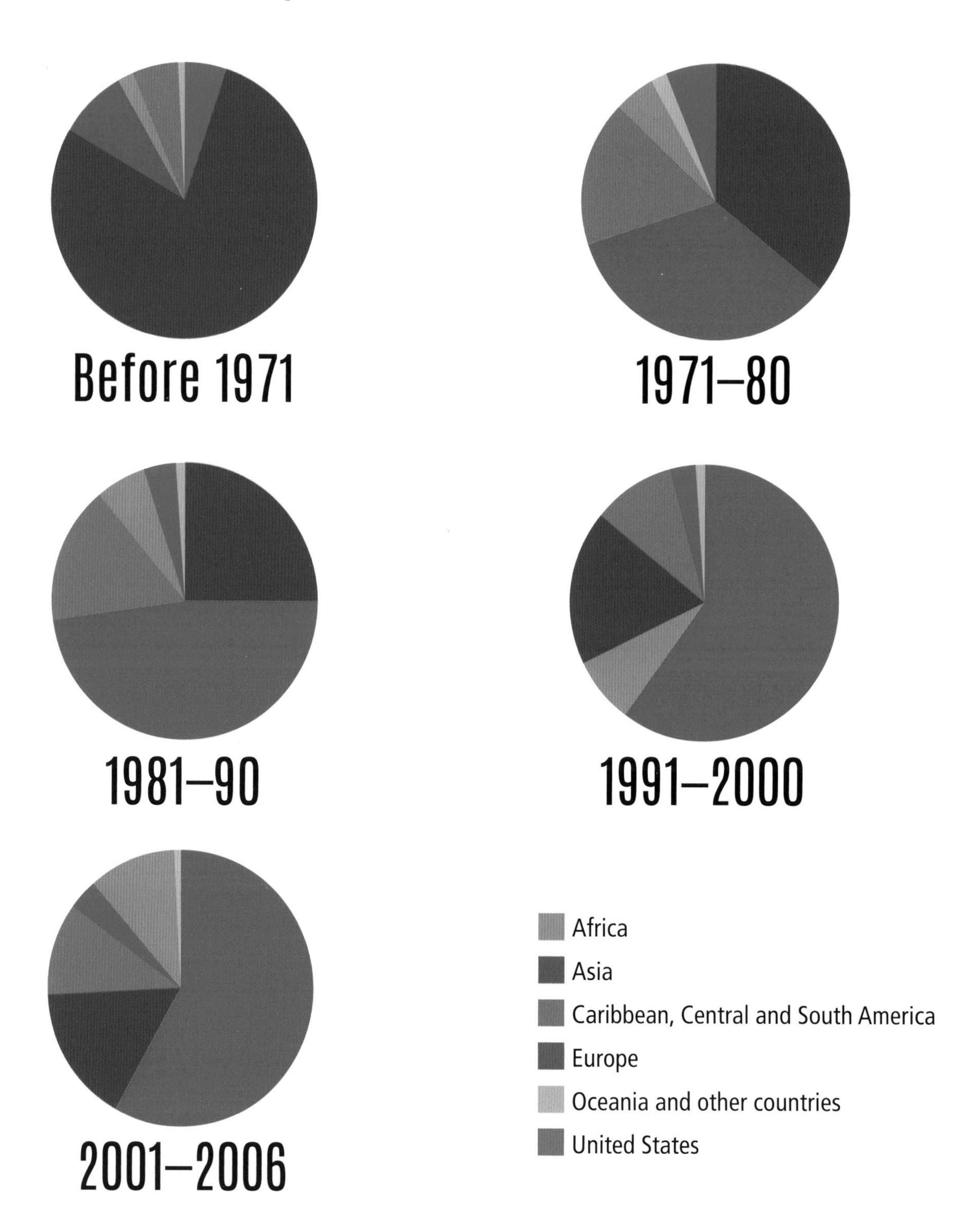

Further Resources

People from every country in the world now call Canada home. This book has introduced you to just some of them. If you want to learn more about immigration and the immigrants who have helped build this country or about your own family's background, here are some online resources that can help.

www.bac-lac.gc.ca/eng/discover/genealogy/Pages/introduction.aspx
Library and Archives Canada's Genealogy and Family History portal can help you begin to trace your family's roots.

www.cic.gc.ca
Explore this Immigration and Citizenship Canada site to find out more about Canadian citizenship, immigration laws, and the refugee system.

www.historicacanada.ca
The Historica Canada website is chock full of information about Canadian history. Check out the minute-long "Heritage Minute" videos to see stories related to the theme of "settling Canada," including the Underground Railroad, the Irish typhus orphans, and building a Prairie soddie. The "Citizenship Challenge" allows you to study for and take a test like the one immigrants must pass to receive Canadian citizenship.

www.thecanadianencyclopedia.ca
The Canadian Encyclopedia is a searchable digital encyclopedia filled with entries relating to the country's history, immigration, ethnic groups, geography, and famous Canadians.

www.canadianhistory.ca/iv
Immigrant Voices offers an informative historical overview of immigration to Canada. The site includes images, maps, graphs, and documents.

www.pier21.ca
Go to the Canadian Museum of Immigration at Pier 21 website to learn more about Canada's immigration history through a research database, individual immigrant's stories and videos, games, and more.

www.bac-lac.gc.ca/eng/discover/immigration/Pages/introduction.aspx
This landing page for Library and Archives Canada's Immigration section has links to many historical documents, information databases, and places for further research. It can connect you with historical documents, photos, and artifacts that illustrate Canada's history of immigration.

www.ourroots.ca
The Our Roots website gives you online access to Canada's local histories.

www.whitepinepictures.com/seeds
A Scattering of Seeds: The Creation of Canada is the website for a television series celebrating the contributions made by immigrants to Canada. You can read about the episodes and watch video clips online.

www.passagestocanada.com
Passages Canada is a digital archive of written and audio stories. Immigrants share their experiences coming to Canada, their path to becoming citizens, and their families' culture and traditions. You can search for stories by theme or by a person's country of origin. You can even share your own story.

Glossary

Aboriginal peoples: Canada's first peoples—First Nations, Inuit, and Métis

citizen: a person who has the legal right to live, work, and vote within a country, and to serve in its military and carry its passport. People born in Canada are automatically Canadian citizens; immigrants who move to Canada must apply to become citizens.

colony: a territory that is controlled by another, often distant, nation; the settlement created by a group of people sent from that nation

Confederation: the official union of three British North American colonies—New Brunswick, Nova Scotia, and Canada—on July 1, 1867, to form a nation called the Dominion of Canada. The dominion had four provinces to start: Ontario, Quebec, Nova Scotia, and New Brunswick.

discrimination: the unfair treatment of people because of differences such as race, culture, religion, or gender

displaced person: the term used until the mid-1900s to describe a person who had been forced from his or her home because of war, natural disaster, or cruelty; today the term "refugee" is used

economy: the system under which wealth and jobs are created in a country by producing goods and services that are bought and sold

homestead: a piece of land that a settler could claim in exchange for living on and farming it for a length of time

human rights: basic rights that belong to every person, including the rights to life, liberty, security, and protection under the law

immigrant: a person who comes to a country to settle

multicultural: a word that describes a society like Canada's, which is made up of many distinct cultures and groups

refugee: someone who is unwilling or unable to return to his or her home country because of war, natural disaster, or fear of torture or other persecution

tolerance: a willingness to accept differences between ourselves and others

Acknowledgements

I wish to thank Niki Walker and Janice Weaver for their tremendous editorial work on this book and Anne Shone for locating so many of the gorgeous visuals that appear in it. I would also like to acknowledge the assistance of the following people: Mohammed Aman; Will Armstrong; Esther Bryan, the Invitation Project; Irvine Carvery, the Africville Genealogy Society; John Hagan; Melynda Jarratt; Marshall-Shibing Jiang; Yanwei (Vivian) Jiang; Les Jozsa; Tomas Kubinek; Prof. Tony Kuzak; Dr. David Lai; Khanh Le, the Vietnamese Association; Diane McCord, the United Empire Loyalists' Association of Canada, Toronto branch; Jinoo Muther; Paul Muther; Elattuvalappil Parvathy; Aly-Khan Rajani, CARE Canada; Michelle Rusk; Ghanesh Sinnappu; Manuela Stefan; Timothy Linh Tran; and Rena Yang.

Photo Credits

Care has been taken to trace ownership of copyright materials contained in this book. Information enabling the publisher to rectify any reference or credit line in future editions will be welcomed.

Alamy = AL

Dreamstime = DR

Glenbow Archives = GA

Library and Archives Canada = LAC

Shutterstock = SH

Front cover: SH (main), LAC/C-046355 (far L), Museum of Vancouver Collection: H990.277.6 (middle L), THE CANADIAN PRESS/Stephen Thorne (middle R), LAC/PA-041785 (far R); back cover: THE CANADIAN PRESS/Jonathan Hayward (L), LAC/s000959k (R); background patterns: DR; 6: SH (top), LAC/C-046355 (bottom L); Museum of Vancouver Collection: H990.277.6 (middle L); © Mark Blinch/Reuters (middle R), LAC/PA-122657 (R); 8: LAC/C-007300; 9: LAC/C-073716; 10: LAC/e008299421; 11: courtesy of the Royal BC Museum and Archives; 12: LAC/C-114480; 13: SH; 14: LAC/C-007300; 15: Rolf Hicker Photography/AL; 16: LAC: C-073709; 17: LAC/C-070232 (top), canadabrian/AL (bottom); 18: LAC/C-073716; 19: LAC/C-020126; 21: LAC/e011154201, The Loyalists by J.D. Kelly 1934. Reproduced with permission of Rogers Communications Cda CAC Inc. (top), LAC/s000959k (middle), © Classic Image/AL (bottom); 23: courtesy of Kings Landing Historical Settlement (top), LAC/C-002001 (bottom); 24: The National Archives, UK (L), LAC/C-040162k (R); 25: LAC/C-115424k; 27: Cincinnati Art Museum, Ohio, USASubscription Fund Purchase/Bridgeman Images (top), ClassicStock/AL (bottom); 28: Africville bicyclists by the railroad tracks, Bob Brooks, photographer, ca. 1965; NSA, Bob Brooks fonds, 1989-468 vol. 16/neg. sheet 7 image 14 (scan 200715065); 29: Passport for Cato Ramsay to emigrate to Nova Scotia, 21 April 1783; NSA, Gideon White family fonds, MG 1 vol. 948 no. 196 (scan 200402028); 30: LAC/PA-041785; 31: LAC/C-086484; 33: LAC/PA-122657 (top), The Jeanie Johnston Company (bottom); 35: LAC/PA-046810 (top), LAC/C-066294 (middle), LAC/C-079029 (bottom); 37: LAC/PA-048475 (top), LAC/e008319005 (middle), SH (bottom); 38: LAC/C-003693; 39: LAC/C-095320k; 41: LAC/e010779321 (top L), GA NA3800-01 (top R), LAC/C-014492 (bottom); 42: LAC/PA-020505 (L); 43: Prisma Bilagentur AG/AL (top), LAC/PA-018151 (bottom); 45: New Iceland Heritage Museum — Gimli, Manitoba (top and middle), GA NA-2438-3 (bottom); 46: LAC/C-003693; 47: LAC/PA-144822 (top), SH (middle); 48: LAC/C-072064; 49: GA NA-3740-29 (top), LAC/e011074369 (bottom); 50: LAC/PA-118195; 51: GA ND-2-109 (top), LAC/C-014118 (bottom); 53: GA NA-3342-2 (top), LAC/PA-123090 (middle), LAC/PA-061139; 54: LAC/C-063256; 55: LAC/C-095320k (top), LAC/e000000739 (bottom); 57: LAC/C-005611 (top), GA NA-4391-1 (middle), GA NA-670-45 (bottom); 58: LAC/PA-178587, LAC/PA-178595; 59: LAC/PA-088459 (top), Zvonimir Atletic/AL (bottom); 60: GA NA-237-9 (L), GA NA-3556-1 (R); 61: LAC/C-056088; 62: City of Vancouver Archives CVA 7-123; 63: LAC/e010753716; 64: LAC/C-137978; 65: LAC/C-081314 (top), LAC/C-029397 (bottom); 66: public domain/Vancouver Public Library; 67: City of Vancouver Archives CVA 7-123 (top), CVA 7-129 (bottom); 68: LAC/e010753716 (L), GA NA-5124-22 (R); 69: LAC/C-046350; 71: LAC/PA-037467 (top), LAC/C-046355 (middle L), LAC/C-057249 (middle R), LAC/PA-134097 (bottom); 73: World History Archive/AL (top), Imperial War Museum (bottom); 74: Canadian Science and Technology Museum; 75: Vancouver Holocaust Education Centre (top), Canadian Museum of Immigration at Pier 21 [D2013.1912.24]; 76: LAC/PA-008179 (L), LAC/PA-175790 (R); 77: LAC/PA-147114; 79: LAC/PA-152023 (top L), LAC/PA-181009 (top R), Danita Delimont/AL (bottom); 80: SH; 81: Jonny White/AL; 82: LAC/e011044970; 83: LAC/e011052358 (top), LAC/e011052346 (bottom); 85: AP Wide World AP (top), Canadian Science and Technology Museum (middle), LAC/C-007108 (bottom); 86: LAC/e001096648; 87: Baldwin Street Gallery; 89: AP Photo/Eddie Adams (top), Fram Museum/public domain (bottom); 91: Matiullah Achakzai/AP Preserver (top), THE CANADIAN PRESS/Stephen Thorne (bottom L), © Mark Blinch/Reuters (bottom R); 92: LAC/e010758222; 93: SH; 94: Megapress/AL; 95: Jonny White/AL; 96: SH; 97: DR (top), SH (bottom); 98: SH; 99: SH (top), LAC/PA-211879 (bottom); 100: SH; 101: Megapress/AL; 102: SH; 103: Ken Gillespie/AL (top), SH (bottom); 104: Corriere Canadese; 105: Sing Tao Daily (top), Indo-Canadian Times (middle), Bizim Anadolu (bottom); 106: Tibor Bognar/AL (L), DR (middle), SH (R); Aurora Photos/AL (top), DR (bottom); 108: DR (top), Chensiyuan/Wikimedia Commons (bottom); 109: SH (top), Don Gunn/Creative Commons (bottom); 111: SH; 112: © Mark Blinch/Reuters (top), DR (bottom L), Fram Museum/public domain (middle), Canadian Science and Technology Museum (bottom R); 128: DR.

Index